SOLUTIONS

STEP BY STEP

A Substance Abuse Treatment Manual

Also by Insoo Kim Berg

Family Based Services

Working with the Problem Drinker (with Scott Miller)

The Miracle Method (with Scott Miller)

Interviewing for Solutions (with Peter DeJong)

A NORTON PROFESSIONAL BOOK

SOLUTIONS
STEP BY STEP
V I D E O T A P E

Substance Abuse Treatment Demonstrations

After reading *Solutions Step by Step: A Substance Abuse Treatment Manual*, you'll want to watch the *videotape* to see the authors in action. Insoo Kim Berg and Norman Reuss work with several different clients to demonstrate many of the techniques discussed in this manual, commenting on each interview in a conversational, yet informative, instructional style. Demonstrations include how to help a man convicted of a DWI see that he has a drinking problem, how to help a couple find a positive way to work out their mutual anger and exasperation, and how to set therapeutic goals in an initial interview.

Published by W. W. Norton & Company, Inc.

To order the *Solutions Step by Step Videotape*, call 1-800-233-4830.

SOLUTIONS
STEP BY STEP

A Substance Abuse Treatment Manual

Insoo Kim Berg & Norman H. Reuss

W. W. Norton & Company • New York • London

Copyright © 1998 by Insoo Kim Berg and Norman H. Reuss

For information about permission to reproduce selections from this book, write to Permissions,
W. W. Norton & Company, Inc., 500 Fifth Avenue, New York, NY 10110.

Library of Congress Cataloging-in-Publication Data

Berg, Insoo Kim.
Solutions step by step : a substance abuse treatment manual /
Insoo Kim Berg & Norman H. Reuss.
p.   cm.

"A Norton professional book."
Includes bibliographical references and index.
ISBN 0-393-70251-0 (pbk.)
1. Substance abuse — Treatment.   2. Solution-focused therapy.

I. Reuss, Norman H.   II. Title.
RC564.B46   1997
616.86'06—dc21   97-18361   CIP

W. W. Norton & Company, Inc., 500 Fifth Avenue, New York, N.Y. 10110
http://www.wwnorton.com
W. W. Norton & Company Ltd., 10 Coptic Street, London WC1A 1PU
2 3 4 5 6 7 8 9 0

To Steve de Shazer, my best friend, colleague, and partner in life.

IKB

To Barbara and my boys, who have put up with my "empty shell" for a long time while my brain has been creating this book.

NHR

Contents

Introduction

The widespread acceptance of managed care has brought an unprecedented challenge to the field of behavioral health care: to rethink what we do. We are under increasing pressure to be innovative, cost-efficient, and client-driven. The solution-focused approach to the treatment of problem substance use described in this book works under these pressures. This model reaffirms our original reason for having entered this field: to restore the integrity and dignity of our clients' sense of who they are and how they want to live their lives. This model also allows us to put this ideal into practice.

All problems, even substance abuse problems, have exceptions; that is, times when the problem could have happened but somehow did not. This solution-focused model is based on this simple idea. Of course, simple is not always easy and it certainly is not simple-minded. We find this is even more so with substance abuse. Most of our clients come to us after years of struggle or repeated failed recovery attempts. But unlike the common myth that alcoholics drink all day and addicts are either in a stupor or on a "jones," they do have times when they have somehow managed to do something different. Discovering the details and helping a client tell rich stories (White & Epston, 1990) about these "exceptions" can be a powerful resource for motivation, encouraging him to believe in himself even when others have written him off as helpless and hopeless.

In clinical practices throughout the United States and Europe we have observed clients making remarkable changes in their lives. Some of these changes seemed too good to be true. A long-time alcoholic would tell us how he got up one morning and just quit. Just stopped drinking, cold turkey, without the benefit of a formal assessment, diagnosis, and treatment plan from an expert. We wondered how this could be. How could clients begin their recovery without our valuable input? So, we asked them, "How did you do this?" They told us remarkable stories about how they rebuilt their lives, step by step. Then we learned these people are called "self changers" (Sobell & Sobell, 1978; Sobell, Sobell, Toneatto, & Leo, 1993) and that there are many professionals who study their healing methods.

This book is about how to capitalize on the strategies of past success and help your clients build solutions in their life. The model we describe comes

Quick Tip:

A Difference that Makes a Difference

Solution building is more effective than problem solving because solution building focuses on a client's resources and successes while problem solving focuses on a client's weaknesses and deficits.

from listening carefully to our clients over the years (de Shazer, 1985, 1988, 1991, 1995; Berg & Miller, 1992; Cabié, 1995; DeJong & Berg, 1997). We listened to their yearnings, desires, hopes, dreams, and even complaints about how we and other professionals have treated them. We also paid attention to their successes, no matter how small or apparently insignificant. In part I of this book, we will guide you through a typical case, from the initial phone call to discharge, one step at a time. In part II, we show you how we use our solution-focused approach in special treatment situations. During this process we will offer many useful quick tips and answer your nagging questions.

For some clinicians, this book will be another step on the journey from a problem-solving approach to the solution-building approach. For those still practicing a traditional treatment approach, this book will present a whole new way of thinking about clients and how they make changes in their lives. Please join us in this adventure of helping clients help themselves.

SOLUTIONS

STEP BY STEP

A Substance Abuse Treatment Manual

PART I

SOLUTION-FOCUSED THERAPY, ONE STEP AT A TIME

Chapter 1

Start by Getting a Head Start

Most clients tell themselves every day that they must stop drinking. For some it is a bedtime prayer that God will please help them stop drinking. For others it is a morning ritual as they stare at their reflection in a steamy bathroom mirror. The fact that today a woman picked up the phone and called us for help was made possible by all the days she didn't. Recovery doesn't begin the day our client visits our office; it doesn't even begin the day she stops drinking. Recovery begins on the day she has the thought for the very first time, "I've got to do something about this drinking." It is prudent to take advantage of this change that happened even before the client picked up the phone to call for help. Even when our client is forced to see us and we are tempted to think she is only calling to placate someone else, such as her husband to stop nagging her, her thinking about and making this phone call is doing something different and it was based on her recognition that previous attempts have failed. Now that something *is* being done, we have to think of ways to take advantage of this important step she has already taken toward her recovery. We call these first steps "pretreatment change," and we want to know as much as possible about how our client has taken these first steps.

Pretreatment change occurs much more frequently than we notice. Moshe Talmon noticed this phenomenon in the late 1980s in his Kaiser Permanente Medical Group clinic in California. To capitalize on it, he began giving a homework assignment between the first phone call and the first office visit. When he did this he increased the number of clients who felt satisfied that they could handle their problems on their own after only a single session (Talmon, 1990). Frequently, clients need only a slight nudge to continue going in the positive direction they started on their own. Sobell and Sobell (Sobell et al., 1993) have studied what they call "self changers." Because these self-changed problem-drinkers have never come to our offices or sought our help, they are unknown to us. The Sobells' findings, however, indicate that even chronic, severe problem drinkers are able to gain control of their drinking and their lives.

Quick Tip:

Capture Presession Change

During a presession telephone call, ask your client to keep track of what is happening in his life that he wants to have continued. During the first meeting with the client, be sure to find out about the details of those things that are worth continuing.

SUBSTANCE USER'S COMPETENCY WORKSHEET

Norm developed the substance user's competency worksheet (see appendix) that can be sent to the client before the first meeting or used as a first-session tool to help clients recognize they have already begun to do something about their substance abuse problem. Here are some suggestions for how to use the worksheet:

1. For those clients who seem unable to read or to understand the instructions, you may need to provide special assistance. We have trained our staff at the intake desk to be sensitive to this and to offer assistance with comments like, "These forms are so complicated" or "You know—this paperwork—they ask for everything under the sun. Do you think you need some help?" or "You have to practically give up your house and firstborn child before you can talk to the counselors nowadays. They ask such dumb questions. Let me know if you need some explanations."

2. For those clients who seem lost or hesitant at filling out essay questions, we find it best to use the recovery checklist (see appendix), where clients can check the items that pertain to their own situation (this is explained below).

3. As the title indicates, the worksheet can easily be used to begin the initial interview by talking about the client's success stories. We find that it often allows us to bypass the lengthy and detailed description of failures, pains, grief, and shame that clients feel obliged to divulge before thinking about possible solutions.

4. When reviewing the worksheet (and checklist), experiment with questions like, "How are you doing that?" "How did you figure out that 'slowing down' your pace will work for you?" "Wow, it's amazing—what made you think of eating fresh vegetables first, before starting to sip your scotch?" "What else did you do so that you told yourself that waiting five minutes for the craving to go away would be helpful?" These kinds of questions in response to the client's worksheet are powerful alternatives to "praise."

INFORMATION GATHERING AS TREATMENT

The most usual means of collecting presession information is the intake form. Along with demographic data, most intake forms ask about the substances the client has used in both the past and present, the current amount and frequency of the substance use, and the client's history of substance use, including all the problems the client has experienced as a consequence of the substance abuse. Once collected, traditional substance abuse treatment professionals do something peculiar with this information. They believe it is all a lie and accuse the client of underreporting the number, amount, and frequency of substances used or minimizing the negative consequences of his or her use. The field of substance abuse (and to some extent the mental health field in general) is the only professional health care discipline that does not trust an optimistic and positive client's self-report. It has been a

• • • • • • • • • • • • • • • • • • • •

Tips from the Field:

A Head Start

When a client calls for a first-session appointment, Insoo's receptionist gives the client the following instructions, "Your appointment will be with Insoo on Wednesday at 2:00 P.M. Insoo would like you to keep track of what goes well in your life between now and when you come to see her."

longstanding tradition to view with suspicion and mistrust the information that clients give. We have evaluated this phenomenon and decided to trust what our clients tell us about their substance use or non-use. This helps us form a collaborative relationship with them. This in turn makes the work go faster and better because we become our clients' partners in treatment.

ASSESSING WHAT THE CLIENT WANTS

In addition to the usual substance use information, we want to know whose idea it was for the client to call for help. Like a construction worker glancing at a blueprint for an overview of the scope of a building project, we glance at the circumstances under which the client has come for help to give us an overview of the treatment. The information helps us determine the client-therapist relationship, which will guide us on what to do and what not to do. There are two common client-therapist relationships: the customer-type and the visitor-type. When the client says he has a problem and wants to fix it or is asking for our help with a family member who has a problem, we know we are in a customer-type relationship with that client. Even when this client has been told he must see us, if it is his idea to see us *now* because of a problem he wants to fix, we are in a customer-type situation. When the client wants us to help someone else, we are still in a customer-type relationship. This client knows his efforts have not netted the results he had hoped for, and is asking for our help in a new effort. This is often the case with parents who have a child who is abusing substances and a spouse who has a partner who is abusing substances. These clients want us to teach them a more effective way to be a helper.

When the client who is calling for an appointment hasn't a clue about why he's calling (he only knows someone—a parent, probation officer, social welfare worker, teacher, etc.—told him he had to make the phone call and get into therapy), we know we are in a visitor-type relationship (Berg, 1994; Berg & Miller, 1992).

Knowing the type of relationship we initially have with our client helps us modulate the pace of our first session. In a customer-type relationship we know the working goal for the first session will be easy to establish and the pace will be quick. Clients in this situation are ready to do something different to make their life, or the life of a loved one, better. In a visitor-type relationship we know we will not have a working goal for the first session and our pace must be gentle and supportive.

Knowing the type of initial situation we have with the client also helps us define some of our therapeutic tasks. Using a solution-focused approach can be discomforting for a therapist. Milton Erickson is recognized as the first solution-focused therapist; when asked about his theory for working with clients, he said he invented a new one for each client (Haley, 1993). Having a solution-focused therapy mind-set means that we are creating the direction of treatment as we go and we may not know exactly where we are going until we get there. Knowing the type of relationship we have with our clients

. . . .

Tips from the Field:

Therapy Must Wait While You Take Care of Business.

Therapists who work in clinics and agencies often complain about the conflicting demands to do therapy faster and fill out all the forms demanded by regulatory bodies and third party payers. They say they cannot possibly do both. We agree. However, we do offer this suggestion. At the beginning, let your client know approximately how many sessions will be allotted to paperwork, then ask, "What will we accomplish over the next three sessions that will give you the idea that coming here was worth your time?" Toward the end of your paperwork ordeal, return to this question by asking, "On a scale of 1 to 10, where 1 is where you were at when we met last time and 10 represents you've met your goal and this time has been worth your while, where are you today?" Now sit back and prepare to be surprised by the answer.

is our security blanket. With all the "not knowing" we must put up with, we at least know it is our job to help customers remain customers and to help visitors sort out what they want to be different about their life. Although referring to a new way of thinking about clinical supervision, Peter Cantwell (Cantwell & Holmes, 1994) calls this clinical perspective, "leading from one step behind." We think this new way of thinking applies to our clinical practice as well. We recommend that therapists start leading from one step behind, using the questions you ask as "a tap on the shoulder" (Berg, 1994). This can begin even before the client enters your office because as we explained in the previous section, the client's journey toward a more desirable life has already begun before the first phone call.

The downside of this kind of assessment is that as clinicians trained in diagnosing and labeling clients, you may quickly begin to think of your visiting clients as "visitors." Unfortunately, this may lower your positive and optimistic expectations for change and you may simply sit around waiting for the client to become a customer. It is very important to stress that "customer" and "visitor" are words that describe the *type of relationship* you have with your client. Understanding this relationship is vital to utilizing all of your skills to help your client develop realistic goals for treatment. We have actually toyed with the idea of referring to visiting clients as "hidden customers" because it implies that all clients want something and it is our job to find out what it is they want.

USEFUL QUESTIONS TO ASK RELATED TO THE REQUEST FOR SERVICES

The following questions are designed to be adapted to each of your clients as guided by your clinical intuition and judgment. As we will say many times, solution building is not a cookie-cutter, one-size-fits-all approach. Each client is a unique experiment-of-one and our questions are designed to help create solutions that are a custom fit. Questions should be tailored for each client: listen carefully to their words and ideas and work them into these questions.

When the client is sent to you for help:

1. Whose idea was it for you to see me today?

2. What makes _____ think that you need to come here?

3. Do you agree with _____'s idea that coming to see me is a good idea?

4. What would have to happen for _____ to say this has been helpful for you?

5. What will _____ do differently when he/she believes you are making these changes?

6. How will that be helpful to you?

7. Are there times now when you are making even small changes?

8. Tell me, how do you do that?

9. What would it take for you to keep making these small changes?

10. Suppose you kept it going for 3/6/9 months, what would be different in your life then?

11. What would your _____ say about how your life would be different then?

12. What would _____ do differently to let you know that he/she notices these changes?

When clients request treatment for themselves:

1. What needs to happen today so you can say it was a good idea to come here?

2. What will be different in your life then?

3. Who will notice most that you have made changes?

4. What will he/she do differently? What difference will that make in your relationship?

5. What else will be different that will let you know you did the right thing by coming to see me today?

6. What can I do to help you get your life in order?

7. What is the first small step you must take to head in the right direction?

8. What would it take to keep you going in that direction?

9. What will you notice is different in 3/6/9 months?

10. How will making these changes today help you then?

RECOVERY CHECKLISTS

Another helpful tool for collecting information on presession change is the substance user's recovery checklist and worksheet (see appendix). Most clinicians are familiar with diagnostic checklists, which are designed to elicit responses that indicate symptoms of a disorder. The Beck Depression Inventory and the Michigan Alcoholism Screening Tool are examples of diagnostic checklists. The recovery checklist is the opposite of a diagnostic checklist: It is designed to elicit responses that indicate symptoms of a solution—exceptions, successes, and pretreatment changes that the client initiated on her own. We use the recovery checklist to discuss our client's initiatives toward her recovery before getting into the "problem talk" (Furman & Ahola, 1992). This enhances our client's self-esteem and motivation to become a cooperative partner for therapy.

How to Use this Recovery Checklist

Notice there are two parts to this recovery checklist. In the first part the client will rate his proficiency on items in five categories common to recovery. The

Tips from the Field:

Enhancing Client Cooperation and Satisfaction

Make a videotape for new clients that explains what your clinic does, how it has helped others, and what clients can expect to go through. Set it up for clients to view while waiting for their first appointment.

Quick Tip:

Therapeutic Relationship

A positive working relationship helps the "medicine go down" but does not produce change. Doing something different is the way to change.

rating scale he will use ranges through five grades from *never* to *always*. Anything checked "1" or more is a successful strategy, since "1" is an improvement over "never." During the conversation, you can refer to these small successes by asking, "I see that you indicated here on item 4 that you are able to avoid situations where you might abuse substances; can you tell me about the most recent episode where you have done this?"

In the second part the client will indicate where a little improvement will make a big difference (we suggest he limit his items to those on the checklist). He may choose any four items without regard to his rating of that item. Some clients choose items they have rated low while others choose items with a high rating. The choice of items is up to the client. Finally, we ask the client to write a brief narrative explaining how improvement in the areas he has chosen will make a difference in his use of substances.

· ·

Questions from the Field:

"Did solution-focused therapy develop to meet the demands of managed care?"

Be careful to maintain a distinction between solution-focused therapy and brief therapy. Many brief therapies have been developed to meet the demands of managed care. Solution-focused therapy was not developed to be brief. This model was developed over 25 years; when we experimented with our ideas we saw our clients make progress rather rapidly. As we refined our techniques the number of sessions decreased. At one point in the development of solution-focused therapy, we purposefully tried to make the therapy longer. This experiment backfired and the therapy actually got shorter. Following the methods we describe will lead to brief treatment without your forcing yourself to do brief therapy.

A WORKABLE GOAL

Before we can go any further in therapy, we need to know what the client considers as termination criteria, a picture of what her life will look like when she has completed treatment. It may seem strange to talk about termination before we even begin, but this lets the client know she is determining the pace and course of therapy. Negotiation of termination criteria must begin before treatment can proceed and it must continue throughout the contact.

When we have a customer-type situation with our client, knowing what the client wants is easy—she tells us. After the client tells us what she wants, we do something that surprises some traditional-minded substance abuse professionals: We go along with it. We think that whatever the client wants is a good place to start therapy. When our client's criteria for termination is limited by external forces such as managed care, which sets a limit on the therapy, we can easily adapt to these limits by starting the conversation like this: "Sixty days from now it will be the end of April. We will be able to get in about eight sessions from now until then. What will be different about your alcohol use 60 days from now?" or "What will be different in your life eight sessions from now that will let you know that you have used this time wisely?"

Sometimes the customer client tells us she wants someone else to change. Someone our client cares about is messing up and she wants us to intervene in some way to make him stop whatever it is he is doing. This is a more difficult situation because we know we cannot make anybody do or stop doing something he doesn't want to stop doing. But we can't tell that to our client right off because that will not help her. We do not want to lecture our client either. Some programs we are familiar with would prefer to lecture this client. They say she is a codependent and has enabled her husband's drinking. They tell her she is just as "sick" as he is and insist she is the one who must be in therapy. We think this is very harsh and not helpful. This lecturing approach does not respect the many times she has tried to do something to help her husband see the damage his drinking is doing. We think it is better to compliment her for caring so much that she was willing to ask for professional help. Then we ask, "Has there ever been a time when you were so frustrated with him you just wanted to scream, but instead you did something different?"

When we have a visitor situation with our client we must take a very different approach. We start with what the client is willing to work for. In the visitor-type relationship our client doesn't have a clue, or he has only a vague notion of why he is being made to see us. He just sits there and says, "Your guess is as good as mine." This is a hard situation for us professionals because it is easy to misunderstand the client and label him as "in denial" and give him a stern lecture. Instead, we do something else. We call whoever sent this client to us and ask her, "What's he doing here?" We are usually told a story about some misdeed that was done while the client was intoxicated or high. The person who referred the client wants this problem cleared up. When we know this story we can ask the client, "Did you know that's why you are here?" When the client says, "Yes," we ask, "Oh, do you want to be here for that?" When the client says yes to this, it usually means he has nothing better to do, but it's a place for us to start, so that's where we start.

Sometimes the visitor client says, "No! Are you crazy? I don't want to be

• •

Questions from the Field:

"What about the mandated client who doesn't want to be in therapy?"

When the therapist asks, "What do you want to get out of therapy?" the mandated client says, "I want my driver's license back, or my probation officer off my back, or my wife to stop nagging me." We think those are all good things to want. It's already progress. You know clients who don't care about any of those things. Some clients will say, "I don't care if I never drive again" or maybe, "I don't care if she leaves me, I'd welcome the peace and quiet." So, when the client tells us he wants something, we are encouraged; we have something to work with and we are at least walking in the same direction.

here for that!" This is a familiar refrain we all have heard before. They usually have been sent to us because their substance use got them into some kind of trouble and they have been sent to us to be fixed. But they do not want to be fixed; they just want to be left alone. So when the client says, "No, I don't want to be here for that!" we say, "It sounds like you just want to be left alone?" "Yes," the client says, "you got it, I just want to be left alone." Now we have a customer-type relationship with an intermediate goal: to be left alone. Our next question is, "So, what do you think it will take for so-and-so to leave you alone?"

● ●

Quick Tip:

Argumentative Clients

In a visitor-type relationship never take the high moral ground by arguing in favor of making prudent (in your view) changes. When the therapist begins to argue in favor of change, the client can only argue against it. How can you tell you are arguing with the client? A sure sign is when you find yourself saying, "Yes, but" or simply, "But . . ." However, you can help the client see the advantages of making some changes by encouraging him to stay the same. When you argue against change (in favor of staying the same) the client's only option is to argue in favor of it.

Questions from the Field:

"Does codependency exist?"

In the late 1980s and the first half of the 1990s there was a rush to hospitalize everyone with insurance whether or not they needed it. It went along with the trend to see pathology everywhere. Everyone who was in a relationship with an alcoholic was seen as an enabler. This had the tragic consequences of blaming the victims of alcoholism. As the addiction treatment field became aware of what it was doing to people, it became popular to see these people as just as sick as the alcoholic. We began to think of these other people as codependents and children of alcoholics. New treatment programs were developed to heal these new victims of the family disease of alcoholism. We would like to set the record straight on our stance on the treatment of ACOAs and particularity so-called codependents.

We oppose the use of these terms and the thinking that goes into labeling them as such. We strenuously object to professionals' tendency to label clients. When professionals use these labels, it is difficult for the client to remember that these labels are just somebody's idea about reality. The professional's label carries the extra authority of an expert. Clients begin to see their efforts to help their alcoholic loved one as her sick, controlling behavior. The wife of an alcoholic begins to understand her loving attempts to help as filled with suffering that causes her to become bitchy and bitter but unable to leave the alcoholic because of her psychological problems.

This pathologizing view has nothing in common with the clinical phenomenon we have observed in our practices. Contrary to the pathology view, our experience is that these spouses, both men and women, have enormous capacity to tolerate frustration with unlimited patience and undying hope for the problem drinker. We have met many spouses and parents who have told us they know their loved one will make it someday. We view these family members as tremendous resources. They have stood by their partner or son or daughter through more detoxes and attempts to quit than any professional can ever give them credit for. These spouses know more about the drinker's problem pattern, hidden strengths, and weaknesses than any professional can possibly know. When we utilize their knowledge, solicit their cooperation, and seek their opinion on what they know will work and not work, the treatment can move along quite quickly.

Chapter 2
Exceptions to Problems

All substance abuse problems have exceptions. We find that the majority of clients with substance abuse problems have numerous exceptions. Exceptions are times when he could have drank, lost his temper, got into a fight, heard voices in his head, or arrived two hours late for work, but somehow managed not to. There are two types of exceptions to the client's problem. The first type of exceptions are those the client creates by something he purposefully does. The second type just seems to happen when the problem does not seem to be so much of a problem. For therapeutic purposes, the most useful exceptions are those that the client creates. In the customer-type situation, when the goal is to stop drinking, exceptions occur anytime the client has felt like drinking (the alcohol was available) and he chose not to drink. Whenever the client has an exception to the problem, it is the therapist's job to mine that exception for details. Our therapeutic mining tools are the questions, Who? What? When? Where? and most important, *How?* Our conversation about the exception is punctuated with the inquiry, "How did you do that?" or "Can you do that again?" or "What would your wife say about how you did that?" and "What would it take for that to happen again?" These questions point our client in the direction of a workable solution, one that is do-able within the client's life circumstances, and is realistic. When the exceptions are deliberate, get the client to repeat them. Accumulated successful exceptions will lead to solutions so your client can stay clean and sober longer (or reduce his drinking and drug use).

Some clients think their exceptions are only the second type; the exceptions seem to be random. For example, the client seeking help for her husband may identify the exception as those days when he does not drink. She may not yet see that another exception is the day she is tempted to be bothered by his drinking but she does something else instead. These exceptions are the building blocks of a workable solution, which is generated from within and not forced by others. When exceptions are not of our client's own doing we are unable to proceed to the creation of a workable solution. In these situations we use the miracle question to continue to develop our client's ideas for the beginning stages of a solution that is achievable.

Questions from the Field:

"What if all the client wants is to get his driver's license back?"

In our view this is a good thing to want. Not all of our clients are willing to do the hard work that the state will require to get their driver's license back. We see this client as very motivated to do whatever it will take. When our client says something like this we know we have a customer-type situation for getting the driver's license. Of course, it takes lots of hard work to achieve that goal, including movement to stop drinking.

THE MIRACLE QUESTION

What is the "miracle question"? We discovered the power of the miracle question accidentally. In the early 1980s, Insoo was interviewing an overwhelmed client who was unable to make progress in therapy. When Insoo asked this client what she thought it would take to make even a small amount of progress, the client answered, "It would take a miracle!" With her insatiable curiosity, Insoo wondered aloud, "Suppose a miracle did happen . . ."

How to Use the Miracle Question

When we ask the miracle question we pay careful attention to three things.

1. We use the word "suppose," drawing attention to it with our facial expression, modulation and tone of voice, and using appropriate pauses to pace the client's images of solutions. We want our client to suspend the day-to-day reality of the problem for just long enough to believe in a reality where the problem does not exist.

2. We do not refer specifically to any problem. We use the phrase "the problems that brought you here" to allow for a solution that is not tied to any given problem. Our experience has taught us that solving problems is very different from creating solutions. On the "miracle day" we want our client to be able to create solutions that are free of restrictions or barriers that limit the client's creating a vision of a problem-free life.

The Miracle Question

"Suppose when you go to sleep tonight (pause), a miracle happens and the problems that brought you here today are solved (pause). But since you are asleep you can't know this miracle has happened until you wake up tomorrow. What will be different tomorrow that will let you know this miracle has happened and the problem is solved?"

3. After we finish asking the question we pause for a very long time. We have noticed that our clients are not used to being asked questions about miracle days. It is a hard question for them to answer. They must give it a lot of thought before answering. Give them time. After you ask the miracle question you may notice your client tilt her head upward as if to search the ceiling for an answer. That is exactly what your client is doing—searching for an answer. Wait it out. When our client says, "I don't know," we have learned to wait just a little longer in silence, as if we did not hear her and do not know it is now our turn to speak. Clients will usually take this as another cue to think harder and come up with a more complete answer. When our clients have persisted with the position of not knowing what will be different on the miracle day, we say, "Guess!" No client has ever been unable to guess. Our conversation about the miracle day is now in progress. The next step is to map out the details of this solution.

Usually when we ask the miracle question the client answers with some unlikely event such as, "Winning a lottery," "Finding the fountain of youth," or "Experiencing eternal happiness." Think of these answers as his way of giving himself some time to imagine truly creative solutions. After a few good laughs, clients usually settle down to describe changes in everyday life, starting with statements that indicate there would be an absence of the problem. To find out what will be different on this miracle day we ask, "What will you be doing instead when you are not . . . ?" On the miracle day clients can easily see that when they are "not . . ." they will be experiencing good feelings. It is helpful to then ask, "When you are feeling (rested) what will you be doing?" or an observation question like, "How will you know you are feeling (rested)?" Simply asking, "What else?" helps to continue the flow of details as we help our clients experience their miracle day. Be sure to include the details of daily interactions by asking questions like, "So when you wake up (rested) what will your wife (dog, children, etc.) be doing that she didn't do this morning?" "When she does that, what will she notice you doing?" and "What else will be happening when the two of you are living a miracle day?"

When the client views the miracle day as someone else changing, for example, "My son will have stopped smoking pot," phrase your follow-up questions differently. Ask, "Suppose your son has stopped using pot; what will he notice is different about you?" or "Suppose your wife has stopped

. . . .

Questions from the Field:

"What do you say to an IV drug user who says that on the miracle day she would wake up without being HIV positive?"

This is a very unhappy situation and we wish we could make a miracle like that come true. We have had clients who have given us this answer. We have also worked with spouses and parents who have wanted a medical miracle for their loved ones. In these situations we think it is best to acknowledge the desire for this miracle. We cannot, however, stop at that; we must move forward by asking, "And on this miracle day when you noticed you were no longer HIV positive, what would you be doing?" and "How would that help?" and "Could doing something like that help now?"

For additional details about working with clients in terrible situations, listen to Insoo's audiotape Dying Well, *which is a conversation with a young woman dying of AIDS (Brief Family Therapy Center, 1992).*

Tips from the Field:

When the Miracle Is a Disaster

At times the client's answer to the miracle question is quite the opposite of what we think will make her life better. For example, the answer to the miracle question is, "My husband, who is a chronic alcoholic, will drop dead." When this happened to Insoo, without missing a beat she asked the woman, "Suppose he did drop dead, which certainly is unlikely, what would you do then that you are not doing right now?" The women paused for a long time and said, "I suppose the first thing I would do is visit my daughter in California." She and Insoo were on the way to creating an alternative future for the client. Clients and therapists can get stopped by the barriers to an imaginative future; however, staying open to getting around the barriers will open up other creative alternative routes to solutions.

drinking, what will she notice is different about you?" Follow up these questions with, "How will that be helpful?" "What else will be different?" "Who else will notice that this is a miracle day?" and "What would your partner do that she didn't do this morning?"

Eventually you will reach the point where the miracle day has been sufficiently explored and described in detail. The use of exception questions will help establish the miracle, such as, "When was the most recent time when small pieces of this miracle were already happening?" Link times in the present context that are related to the client's working goal. Follow up any indications that the miracle is already happening with who, what, when, where, and how questions. The implication is that the client is already making solutions happen.

In the rare event that there is no foreshadowing of the miracle day in our client's day-to-day life we ask, "What would you have to do more of to make even a small part of this miracle day come true?" For the client who does not yet see himself as part of the solution we may ask, "What would have to happen more often for this miracle to take place?" To keep our client pointed in a positive direction we always use the words "more of" to indicate we know something is already happening that can be helpful, instead of emphasizing how far he has to go. When the client is encouraged in this manner, it is easier to maintain the motivation.

When working with relationships, such as a husband and wife or parent and child, the people involved often see the problem differently. When we ask the miracle question, it helps clients to explore new possibilities for solutions. As they move away from their problem focus, they tend to stop blaming each other and begin to see what they have in common. Instead of viewing their relationship as nothing more than a complex set of problems, the

•••

Questions from the Field:

"Doesn't the miracle question encourage a codependent to continue believing that she can do something to change her alcoholic husband?"

When the client's answer is that her miracle day is the day her husband stops drinking, we do not challenge this. It is not useful or helpful to say, "See! You are just as sick as he is. You need to stop thinking in this dysfunctional way." We have found it better to ask two questions: "When your husband stops drinking what will he notice you doing differently?" followed by, "What will you have done to do that?" These questions lead her to the conclusion that she can make some changes even before he makes any changes. This approach enhances her sense of control of her life, not his life, and you are intervening into their relationship.

miracle question helps them view themselves and their family members as affording some possibilities for change.

When we ask the miracle question of a couple or family, we try to limit the discussion to one miracle. With each person we use all the variations of relationship questioning: "After the miracle, what will you notice is different about you?" "What will your parent (spouse) notice is different about you?" "What do you suppose people in your family will be doing differently then?" "How will all of you make that happen?" "What will it take to make a change like that?" and "What will they notice is different about you when they make a change like that?" As with the individual client, exception-type questions are used to establish a bridge from the miracle day to day-to-day life, to imply that our clients have already begun to create their own solutions. To help our clients continue in this solution-focused direction we ask, "What would have to happen for you to do more of that or to do it more often?" and "What would you say it will take to make that happen?"

• •

Questions from the Field:

"My question is about mandated clients from the criminal justice system who were under the influence at the time of the crime. How do you work with them when they just keep saying, "I've learned my lesson" and "I will never do it again"?

We have learned that when we directly confront our mandated client the results are not therapeutic. The mandated client will usually just dig his heals in and refuse our efforts to make progress or become so insincerely compliant with our demands that we are not making a difference. We make a distinction between compliance and change. Prisons value compliance. We value change and hold people responsible for their own change. Ask the client questions that challenge him to become aware of his own process of change. We will ask the mandated client when he tells us he has learned his lesson, "How do you know that?" or "What tells you that you have learned your lesson?" or "How can your partner tell that you learned your lesson and that you will never do it again?" We follow up our question with more questions that call for much detail. We will also ask our mandated client for exceptions by first acknowledging his perception that therapy is unnecessary (because he has already learned his lesson) and saying, "Tell me about a time when you wanted to harm someone and very easily could have harmed him but you didn't." This seems to ease his defensiveness, as he becomes curious about his own control.

SCALING QUESTIONS

A scale of 1 to 10 is used to concretize the client's own assessment of motivation, hopefulness, progress, confidence, the problem, and a host of other factors related to his solutions to substance abuse. Unlike most 1-to-10 scales, we use the numbers to replace the word descriptions (de Shazer & Berg, 1992). We find the scaling question very flexible and infinitely adaptable since anyone who knows numbers can easily answer questions on a 1-to-10 scale. The most useful questions you can adapt immediately are scaling questions your clients can use to assess their own situation. Our follow-up questions help them make their own decisions about the next step to take, thus enhancing their motivation and willingness to continue building solutions.

We have used scaling questions with all our clients in all age groups on a wide range of topics. Children who are old enough to understand numbers can be asked scaling questions as though they were adults. With children who are younger than kindergarten age or who have developmental difficulties, we substitute pictures for numbers.

Scaling questions are also useful when there is disagreement between people. Rather than focusing on the disagreement we ask, "Let's say 1 stands for the most the two of you have ever disagreed about this and 10 stands for a time when you both absolutely agree, where are you today on the scale?" We follow our scaling question with a solution-building question like, "When you are one point higher on the scale, what will the two of you be doing that you are unable to do now?" Clients usually tell us they will be doing more things together and will give us an example of a time when they experienced a happy ending after resolving a disagreement. Of course we want to know how.

We also use scaling questions for assessing progress, confidence, hopefulness, self-esteem, presession change, investment in a relationship, willingness

> ### The Scaling Question
>
> A scaling question asks the client to evaluate either a problem or a solution on a scale of 1 to 10. The template we use for our problem scaling question is, "On a scale of 1 to 10, where 1 represents the problem as bad as it's been for you and 10 represents that time when you are no longer concerned about this problem, where are you today?"
>
> The template we use for our solution scaling question is, "On a scale of 1 to 10 where 1 represents your solution is just a very small idea of what has to happen and 10 is you are actively involved in your own recovery, where are you today?"

• •

Tips from the Field:

The Scaling Question without Numbers

A preschool teacher's aid uses this chart to help a child who is prone to violent outbursts to recognize his feelings. When the child has identified a facial expression, the aid asks, "What would it take for you to go from here (pointing to the face the child identifies) to here (pointing to the face to the immediate right of the identified face)?" and follows the child's answer with the question, "When you get there what will your mother (father) do differently?" Another question that can be useful to inspire the child to move in a positive direction is, "How long do you need to stay here before you are ready to move to the next step?"

to work toward a solution, and difficulty of implementing a treatment plan. This has been adapted to use in the assessment of suicide lethality. Fourteen-year-old Marie came to our attention because of her attempted suicide by overdosing on her mother's tranquilizers. The treatment plan following her week of hospitalization was to continue in outpatient family therapy. Because her mother was quite shaken up by the experience and wanted to know whether she could "put my guard down or do I have to walk on eggshells," we asked Marie to assess her own situation.

> INSOO: Let's say 1 stands for we have to take you back to the hospital right now and 10 stands for your mom and I don't have to even think about it. Where would you say you are right now?
>
> MARIE: (Pause) Umm, I would say about 7.
>
> INSOO: That's great! What will your mother see you do when she believes you have moved from 7 to 8?

Once our client has become accustomed to our scaling questions we begin to use them by simply asking "On a scale of 1 to 10 where are you?" leaving the definitions of 1 and 10 up to them. Of course the scale is a meaningless exercise until we ask our client, "What will it take to move from 3 up to 4?" We use the scaling question as a jumping off point to develop a solution.

Another practical and helpful use of the scaling question is for assessment. We use scales to assess our client's progress in therapy. By noting in the client's chart where he or she is on the scale during the first session and asking a follow-up scaling question a few sessions later, we can see what progress has been made. Our clients are often surprised when we share the two ratings; they suddenly can see that they are making progress.

Managed care companies are also interested in our use of scales for assessment. Therapists often talk to managed care companies in a language that is filled with "vague feeling talk." It is hard to measure progress with feeling talk. When we use the numbers our clients report on their progress scales, we have a more concrete language to use when requesting authorization for additional visits. Numbers are a universal language and everybody understands that numbers on a scale can move up or down and that it is not static. We have even persuaded some managed care companies to accept our scales as the treatment goal, for example, the treatment goal is for

• •

Questions from the Field:

"Do you refer clients to AA?"

Of course, if they are open to it. In this day and age it is rare that the client has never heard of AA. When our client has past experience with AA, we ask, "What did you find helpful about AA?" and "How have you been putting that to use in your daily life?" We add this to our inventory of what has worked for him. Any success he has had by using AA principles is certainly worth repeating and we encourage him to do so. If the client found AA not very helpful, we then ask what he thinks will be helpful instead.

the client to report they are at an 8 on a scale of the solution to the problem that brought them into therapy.

THE NIGHTMARE QUESTION

Only after our attempts to build a solution using questions about presession change, exceptions, and miracle days do we give ourselves permission to ask the "nightmare question." Norm created the nightmare question when he met some clients who were not motivated to make changes by seeing the possibility of life getting better. It seemed to him that some problem drinkers were waiting for something devastating to happen before they would do anything, or they still believed that they could escape the long-term consequences of drinking. However, the more questions he asked the more he noticed the predicament that quitting created for these hard-core problem drinkers. Faced with continued drinking, which placed their jobs in jeopardy, or quitting, which placed all their friendships in jeopardy, these alcoholics did not see abstinence as a solution, but as just another "damn problem."

Follow-up to the nightmare question is similar to that with the miracle question, only in reverse. With the nightmare question we are using problem talk to build a solution our client can live with. In our experience of asking about miracles and nightmares, our clients usually answer the miracle question with a feeling (usually positive and hopeful) and the nightmare question with a behavior (usually a drinking one). When we use follow-up questions to ask for details of the nightmare day we usually start by asking about feelings: "When your wife sees you drinking in the morning what will she notice is different about how you feel?" and "When she sees you feeling this way, what will you notice is different about how she feels?" The simple but powerful question, "What else?" encourages our clients to add more detail. As with the miracle question, if the nightmare is happening to someone else we usually phrase our follow-up questions differently: "When this nightmare is happening to your husband, what will he notice is different about you?" We phrase our questions in this way to draw attention to the effects the nightmare has on everyone, thereby heightening the effect the nightmare may have.

When all the details of the nightmare day have been explored, experiment with bridging questions to help establish a link to possible solutions. You can ask, "Are there times now when small pieces of this nightmare are happening?" "What is the nightmare like during those times?" "Who is most effected by the nightmare when it happens?" and "Who is most interested in seeing to it that the nightmare is prevented?"

To continue building the bridge to possible solutions we ask, "What would it take to prevent this nightmare from happening?" and "How confident are you that you can do what it will take?" For our clients who are still unsure about changing their current behaviors, at least they now know what is in store for them in their future.

When we ask the nightmare question with couples or families we try to have only one nightmare at a time. When we do get two simultaneous nightmares we use questions that ask about human interactions to indicate how separate nightmares affect everyone. "When she is living her nightmare and you are living yours, what will you notice about each other?" "How will these nightmares destroy what you have both been working for?" With couples and families the nightmare question can help them externalize the problem. When clients see "the problem" as the real problem, they can stop blaming each other and begin to create a solution that is good for everyone.

Remember, the nightmare question is a very specialized form of problem talk in solution-focused therapy. We use it to help our clients create solutions only after we have explored pre-session change, exceptions, and miracle days and found them ineffective. When you use the nightmare question we encourage you to persist with your client's perception of what his own nightmare is, instead of giving up on him as a hopeless case.

• •

Questions from the Field:

"Is the nightmare question the same as allowing the client to hit bottom?"

We believe it is unethical not to use these useful techniques and sit by waiting for the client to "hit bottom." Helping the client imagine hitting bottom is safer than allowing them to actually hit bottom.

Even though we do not use the traditional model of "intervention" as described by Vernon Johnson, when the opportunity presents itself to intervene into the client's life we use the situation to point him in a more positive direction. Unfortunately we have met with many clients who have been destroyed by good intentions that went bad in the course of a structured intervention when well-meaning professionals and family members tried to force something down the drinker's throat. As mentioned elsewhere in this text, we by no means turn our back on the efforts of family members to get the drinker sober. We will ask the family members about what they know about the client that keeps them hanging in there after many disappointments and unkept promises. We find this inevitably leads to a discussion of the client's potential and the family's hopes and dreams for him. Hearing this kind of positive view of himself can often be a powerful "intervention" that forces the client to adopt a more positive and optimistic view of himself.

Insoo was once "forced" to have an intervention with a young man. It seems his high school friend and girlfriend flew into Milwaukee for an intervention. The girl was only able to sit and sob throughout the session. The focus of the conversation was on the faith and hope they both had for this young man. This faith and hope was strong enough to make them fly a long distance to tell him they knew he could actually put his life together. It was quite an emotional experience for the client who didn't know how much they each cared about him.

Questions from the Field:

"When clients are in denial do you tell them what their night-mare will be?"

We have not found the idea of "denial" to be very helpful. When therapists we supervise talk about a client being in denial, we find it usually means the client and the therapist are in disagreement about the construction of a problem or the best method to reach the client's goal. We have learned from these situations that a client who is said to be in denial is simply noticing different things and weighing them differently than we do. We have always urged therapists to adopt the client's point of view and frame of reference (DeJong & Berg, 1997), since we are dealing with the client's reality, not ours. When a therapist tells a client what the nightmare will look like, it is no longer the client's nightmare and consequently loses any potential therapeutic value. It is also likely the client has already heard all the dire consequences from someone else.

COPING (GETTING BY) QUESTIONS

Because therapists often encounter clients who are not making any progress at all, we are asked what we do in those instances when nothing the therapist does seems to make a difference in the client's motivation. We want to remind you of something you already know: No matter how caring, compassionate, smart, and genuine you are, if the client does not want to change, there is nothing you or anyone can do to stop destructive behaviors such as substance abuse. Only the client can do it. We do, however, have a few helpful suggestions.

Instead of the common practice of "throwing the bum out" until he "hits bottom," we recommend that you try "coping questions" while you are waiting for your client to be ready for change. Coping questions ask, "How have you managed to come this far without killing yourself with your booze?" When you ask this question, you are likely to be met with a blank stare because he has never been asked this type of question before. Clients are usually told what they are doing wrong. You might notice that the client may be silent for a long time and then begin to answer something like this:

CLIENT: Well, I don't know, I just get through each day.

THERAPIST: I know it's not easy to just get through each day when you have as many problems as you have. So, how do you do it?

CLIENT: Like I said, I just do the best I can each day.

THERAPIST: So, how do you decide what's best for you each day?

Tips from the Field:

Origins of Denial

You have heard that beauty is in the eye of the beholder. We have come to understand that denial is in the theory of the therapist.

CLIENT: You know, it's not easy, doing as much drinking as I do.

THERAPIST: (With curiosity) I'm sure it's not easy. I wonder how you do it?

CLIENT: Actually it doesn't seem like much, but I do try to cut down on my drinking every now and then.

THERAPIST: Wow, how do you do that? I wonder how come you don't drink more?

In our view, not getting any worse takes a significant amount of effort. Imagine running all day on a treadmill. At the end of the day you would be in exactly the same place as when you started but you would have used a great deal of energy. We imagine many clients feel like this; they are running all day but at the end of the day they are in the same place as when they started. Without seeing any progress in their life they get discouraged. When the people around them give them lectures about how their life is going nowhere, they get even more discouraged. We use the coping question to draw attention to all the energy the client is using just to keep from getting worse. When the client can appreciate how much he is really doing, even though not much progress is being made, he is in a better position to make some changes that will capitalize on the energy he is already using. Imagine how far you could run when you get off the treadmill and run on solid ground.

Here is a list of useful coping questions to ask about the seriousness of the problem, that act as triggers for self-reflection on the client's own recovery:

1. On a scale of 1 to 10, where 1 stands for the worst period in your life when you felt like life could not go on any longer and 10 stands for the day after the miracle, where would you say you are right now, between 1 and 10?

2. If I were to ask your family, where would they say you are on that same scale?

3. How do you explain it to yourself that you have come all the way up to 2 (use client's number) already?

4. What would your family say you have done to come up to 2?

5. What would it take to go up just another half-point, to 2.5?

6. What would be different in your life when you move up to 2.5?

7. What will you be doing then that you are not doing now?

8. How will doing that be helpful to you?

9. What will your family notice that will let them know it's helpful to you?

10. What will you have to do to keep this progress going?

Questions from the Field:

"This model seems so contrary to AA principles. How can it work?"

We see this model as having a lot of similarities with AA as described in the Big Book. *The* Big Book *was written as a description of what worked for Bill Wilson, Bob Smith, and the early members of the AA fellowship. These descriptions were never meant as an explanation or prescription. In fact, the AA principles advocate that AA members refrain from offering expert opinions about alcohol problems or offering a prescribed cure-all. In the early days of AA the illness or disease part of alcoholism was not emphasized. Lifelong abstinence was also not a focus of the meetings. Bill Wilson learned from his own experience of many relapses that his focus must be on one day at a time. The concepts of lifelong abstinence and disease theory was advanced by the second generation of AA and the professionals who coattailed on the success of AA.*

We see that our approach and that advocated by the founders of AA as similarly pragmatic. We are interested in doing more of what works. We are also interested in keeping recovery as simple as possible. We do not see that we are in conflict with AA. In fact, we believe we have many more similar philosophical and pragmatic approaches with the original AA philosophy, than we do differences.

Chapter 3
The Client's Workable Solution

We believe the only solution that will work for our clients is the solution they create, not the solution created by the experts. This is a radical idea in the field of addiction treatment. For a long time, professionals in our field believed it was their job to tell people what they must do to become sober. In the AA program it is common to hear a know-it-all say, "The only thing you have to change is everything, starting with people, places, and things." It follows from this view that the experts in the field would insist that their clients do what they say or risk a horrible relapse and eventual death (Johnson, 1973). We have never thought that this was a very helpful approach. In our experience clients will do what they want to do and say, "To hell with the experts." Many studies show that most successful treatments are based on clients making choices. Clients will drop out of therapy when the therapist does not listen and help them in the way they want to be helped. We listen carefully to our clients to learn what has already worked, even if just a little, and get them to do more of that. This enhances client motivation. When we listen and learn that nothing the client has done worked, we continue to search for what might help by asking the miracle and nightmare questions. We have also found it helpful to see family members as resources in building solutions. When we have asked family members what strengths they see in the problem drinker that gives them hope for successful recovery, we have been rewarded with a rich variety of possible solutions and exceptions that document their hope.

Once someone has been labeled "alcoholic," she is seen as either enabling the addiction or attempting to deny the addiction. The successful surgical practice of a medical doctor with a drinking problem is seen as a cover-up for the drinking. We think this pathologizing of the individual is short-sighted. There are many important things that problem drinkers do that has nothing to do with the addiction. For example, they keep their jobs for years and show up on time for scheduled appointments and conferences. When we ask our clients and their families about other hard problems they have solved and about how they have done so, we are again rewarded with a rich history of successes. Our clinical experiences tell us that most problem drinkers lead lives that are far from "unmanageable"—our clients also tell us that because of their problem drinking they have had to manage their lives even more carefully. While the medical model of addiction sees this as "control," we see it as an opportunity to do even more of something that is already working, as a way to change by eliminating or modifying the problem drinking rather than compensating for it. Anything the client does that works should be repeated.

When Norm was presenting the concept of workable solutions during a meeting with a group of clinical supervisors from various addiction treatment facilities, he was interrupted with, "That's nonsense. No one in his right mind would let an alcoholic decide what's going to keep him sober. As they say in AA, it was his *best thinking* that got him drunk!" In our view it is this kind of thinking that leads to so much burnout in addiction therapists. Most of our clients come to us with a variation on the same goal: They want to make their life better. Some of our clients think their life will be better when they stop drinking. Some want to cut down on the booze. Others want someone else to change as a way for life to be better. Still others seem to want the sun and the moon before they will be satisfied that life is finally worth living.

We think any goal the client presents is a good starting point. The fun and excitement in therapy comes from helping people build solutions. Solutions are the surprise and variety in therapy that keeps us interested in helping people. Whenever we hear a therapist say she is burnt out we know it is because she has stopped building solutions with her clients and has been forcing them to go in certain directions. When each session has become a dull routine of the same old thing, it is up to the therapist to provide the wake-up call to the client and get solution building underway.

Goals are what our clients bring to the session; solutions are what we create cooperatively with our clients. When our client tells us, "I want to stop drinking," we do not say, "Okay, this is what you must do." The workable solution will come from the client's answers to our questions about what has already worked and what might be different when given a good second try.

Questions from the Field:

"When I know my clients will benefit from meditation, should I teach it to them?"

Therapists know many good things that will help their clients. We suggest you hold off on making these good suggestions until after you have asked the client for her good ideas about making changes. For example, you may believe that once your client tells you she wants to be more relaxed, it is your job to jump in and teach them relaxation skills. We do not believe this is helpful because this is not the client's idea and the client may or may not follow your suggestion. We think it better to explore with our clients ways they are already relaxing that do not involve problem drinking. Even hard-core problem drinkers have some way to relax when they go on the wagon. We advocate that therapists be on the lookout for what is already working and get the client to repeat that.

Following are some guidelines for a well-formed solution:

1. The client knows how it will help.

2. It is described as the presence of a behavior or the start of something positive or healthy.

3. It is taking the first small step, or continuing the first small step.

4. It is understood by both the client and the therapist as something that will or can make a difference.

5. It is described in specific, concrete, and measurable terms.

6. It is realistic, that is, the client can do it.

7. It is perceived by the client as involving hard work on his or her part.

ABSTINENCE VS. CONTROLLED DRINKING

Twenty-five years after the Sobells (Sobell & Sobell, 1978) launched the greatest debate in the field of alcoholism treatment, the battle continues between the scientific community and the belief-based view of alcoholism. We do not intend to contribute to either side of this debate. Our view is pragmatic and concerned with what works. Mostly abstinence works (Hester & Miller, 1989; Orford, 1985, Orford & Edwards, 1977). Even approaches that allow for both abstinence and moderation maintain better long-term results with abstinence. Therefore, whenever a client wants to stop drinking we encourage it as a prudent course of action. However, there are many convincing studies that challenge an abstinence-only approach. The variables most often mentioned in the literature (severity of dependence and abstinence versus moderation) appear to be independent of success when comparing outcomes (Foy, Nunn, & Rychtarik, 1984; Rychtarik, 1987, Sanchez-Craig, 1983).

So, when our client says, "I don't want to stop completely, just cut down," we do not panic and give him a stern lecture.

Tips from the Field:

Looking for the "Teachable Moments"

There is a great deal of value in educational information as a tool for change. How this information is delivered makes a world of difference in the way the listener accepts the information. The more respectful and collaborative the teacher is, the more likely the listener will hear the message.

Start by asking, "Has anybody told you about what alcohol does to your body?" or "What have you noticed about how alcohol affects your body?" or "What have you been told about the effects of pot on you?" When you pay attention to the client's answers, these questions can pique a client's curiosity and prepare him to be in a more receptive frame of mind. He may even look interested by leaning forward. This is a "teachable moment" during the therapy session.

We have also found that just after we compliment the client during the message we deliver toward the end of the session (just prior to the homework assignment) is another opportunity to share useful information. First ask permission by saying, "During the interview I noticed your curiosity about how alcohol has affected you and I'm wondering if you would like more information from some of my resources?" When the client says, "Yes," you have created a teachable moment.

One of the facts of life that professionals in the addiction treatment field have been reluctant to acknowledge is that in the battle between abstinence and moderate (control) drinking there is no "best" strategy. More than any other single factor, client preference is still the best predictor of successful outcome, particularly with reference to abstinence versus moderate use treatment goals (Isabaert & Cabié, 1997). When our client's goal is to cut down on his drinking we build solutions from what he has tried that has already worked and what else might work when given a good try. What we find clinically is that clients change their minds later and decide to abstain once they experience the benefits of life without drinking.

THE CHOICE APPROACH: FLEXIBILITY IS THE BEST MEDICINE

When we began using solution-focused therapy with our clients, we quickly discovered the need for the broadest and most flexible range of treatment programs possible. The usual approach to a treatment program, which insists that all clients start at one point and finish at another—the expert decides where, seemed to quickly fall apart. When we incorporated our clients' goals and solutions into our treatment plans, we found it difficult to plug them into the traditional treatment slots that correspond to a diagnosis, a fixed stage of recovery, and a packaged treatment plan. Our clients were not beginning at the beginning, proceeding through the middle, and stopping at the end of our continuum of care. Our client's solutions covered a broad range, from the most traditional AA 12-step model to some novel, creative, even unusual solutions. We had clients whose solutions were appropriate for a continuing recovery group, even though they hadn't been through an intensive outpatient program (or any other recovery program).

The only workable way is to design a program that is flexible and broad enough that it can be customized to take advantage of clients' resources. We advocate a menu approach. Using this approach, a variety of options, including individual, couples, family, therapy groups, support groups, detox services, intensive outpatient groups, day treatment groups, and inpatient rehabs, can be presented to the client for mixing and matching. When this menu of services is cyclic rather than linear, your

---

Choice Model in Bruges, Belgium

Dr. Luc Isabaert, the director of psychiatric and substance abuse treatment at St. John's Hospital in Bruges, reports on an innovative and successful choice model that is carried out in three weeks.

Regardless of the severity of the alcohol abuse, all patients check in for a one-week inpatient program. Many become detoxed during this period. Patients are allowed to make choices during this first week as to whether to follow an abstinence or moderate drinking program. During the second week of treatment, patients choose between inpatient or outpatient stay, and individual, group, couples, or family treatment. These choices continue through the third week of treatment. St. John's Hospital has found that many patients change their minds on the focus and modality of treatment during the treatment period. Two-and five-year follow-up studies show impressive data.

client can start and finish the program in a way that makes sense, given his unique goals and solutions.

The impetus needed to get a menu of services off the ground in a managed care or agency setting is resource-sensitive program development. As we all know, the delivery of health care has changed dramatically over the past decade. The funding sources for alcohol treatment demand accountability.

> ### *Successful Menu Approach at Community Health Plan*
>
> Community Health Plan's substance abuse treatment program in the Hudson Valley, New York, area has successfully used a menu approach for all outpatient services for over one year. Faced with underutilization of its groups, the staff redesigned a traditional program into a pick-and-choose menu. Participation in the groups as well as customer satisfaction improved. This innovation has been incorporated into the design of both substance abuse and mental health programs throughout CHP's staff model clinics.

Insurance companies no longer simply authorize alcohol treatment based upon a diagnosis; they want to see a thoughtful treatment plan from a program with a track record. Government funding sources are faced with severe budget cuts and will no longer be able to fund programs on the basis of a sound theoretical model. Outcomes drive the decisions on which programs get funded and which do not. In short, programs are being forced to conserve their resources, something clients have had to do all along. Our clients are experts in resource conservation. They know approximately how much money they can afford to spend on making changes, how much time, energy, and people power they have to make recovery happen. We must use this expertise in the planning of our programs to maximize the impact we can have with our clients. We must have programs that fit our client's needs and be able to quickly move clients into those programs.

A menu of treatment options cannot, however, stand alone. A flexible program of treatments can only remain flexible when it is supported by a system that has decentralized the decision-making responsibilities from upper managers to clinical line staff and developed accessible and rapid pathways for implementation.

In the traditional model of program development the experts designed the programs because they knew what was best for the clients. In the new resource-sensitive, collaborative approach, the decision of what is best for the client is made jointly. The client, working with a therapist, constructs a solution, which then is used to form a treatment plan by combining the resources of the client with the resources of the treatment program. This is a very dynamic process, subject to many permutations from beginning to end. System managers must focus their attention on the maintenance of decentralized and flexible programs so that program managers can quickly respond to the changing expectations of user groups (therapists, clients, employers, managed care gatekeepers).

Program managers must also be able to implement decisions about program treatment offerings in a timely manner. This calls for the system to develop implementation pathways that are available, easy to access, and easy to navigate. We believe that without such organizational structure and flexibility of the service delivery system even the most effective treatment model, such as described here, would be difficult to implement. The burden of efficiency and effectiveness does not rest solely on the client or the therapist.

Often forgotten in the discussion of resource management are the employers. These are the people most responsible for our paychecks. Managed care is currently thriving in the United States because traditional indemnity insurance plans and traditional treatment has not addressed employers' demands for efficient and effective treatment. Employers also expect productivity from their employees and from the treatment community. Employers measure a treatment's effectiveness by employee productivity, decreased rehab stays, reduced frequency and intensity of employee on-the- job problems, and cost conservation. We must recognize that a partnership for resource management must be formed between the client, the provider, and the employer. Employers' needs are no longer tangential to treatment planning—they are a central partner in the process. In our view this not only makes good business sense, but also good clinical sense. Forming a partnership between these parties gives our clients a voice in treatment decisions that effect their future and their resources.

• •

Chapter 4

Homework

When the client's workable solution and the program options come together, we have a treatment plan. Homework is the treatment plan in action in the client's real-life environment. In solution-focused therapy, homework assignments must be logical and reasonable, and they must make sense to the client. When our client has already begun a solution, the homework is to do more of what is already working. In fact, the best homework assignment is the simple task of doing more of what is already working. What could be more logical than that?

• •

Questions from the Field:

"Years ago I was involved with a group of strategic therapists and got turned off by the elaborate homework tasks. It seemed to me that they were trying to manipulate the clients. How is this different?"

You are probably referring to the work of many strategic therapy approaches that saw homework assignments as the key to solutions to presenting problems. They saw the client's solution as the problem that they had to get rid of and replace it with a behavior the therapist and the team saw as more functional. This required a lot of clever homework tasks and much manipulation. Your observations were accurate. We do not make the assumption that the client's solutions are a pathological response so we do not have to manipulate our clients into being good. In our view many of the client's solutions are already good, so we just want them to do more of what is already working. We are trying to help good people be better.

DO MORE OF WHAT WORKS

When you tell the client to keep doing something that is already a successful solution to his problematic use of substances, you are using the simplest, easiest, and most effective tool to build success. This suggestion is the most frequent homework assignment we give. In order to arrive at a point where we can make this suggestion to a client we must have conversations with him to uncover the many useful strategies he is already using. We cannot emphasize strongly enough that the tone and nature of these conversations are such that exceptions to the problem, anything that is worthy of repeating, are uncovered and articulated.

DO THE EASIEST, DO THE SIMPLEST

When the client's solution is new to them we suggest that he do the easiest of what might work. It is not uncommon for clients to have several good ideas about what they want to do to reach their goal. Many have been told by both family and friends what they must do to get their life in order. We have found that even though many clients did not follow the advice given to them, they always seem to remember it. When some of this advice comes out in therapy as good ideas for things to do, we help our client prioritize the ideas on a scale of what might make the most difference for the least effort. Clients are not fools; they know change is going to take a great effort. When we acknowledge this by prioritizing tasks for economy of effort and maximum gain, they know we understand how difficult it is to make changes. When we have agreement on the degree of difficulty, we will ask our client to make the easiest, simplest, and smallest change on the list either on a daily basis or randomly as determined by a flip of a coin.

• •

Tips from the Field:

General Rules for Homework

Generally, homework falls into two types: Do more of what works and do something different when the attempted solutions do not work.

1. *Move from smaller to larger, simpler to more complex tasks.*
2. *Suggest tasks that involve active effort on the part of the client, but not exotic tasks that are far from their usual way of life.*
3. *Be clear and specific; take time to develop the assignment.*
4. *All assignments should be no-fail; even when a client does not do the homework assignment, think about the useful aspects of whatever the client did between sessions.*
5. *Try calling the homework an experiment.*
6. *Remember that you have prescribed homework.*

There are those rare occasions when we arrive at the end of the session and all the possible solutions just do not fit our client's goal. This is when our experience working with other clients can pay off. We can make suggestions to our client based on what has worked for other clients in similar situations. This kind of educational approach can prove very useful when it is done in a sincere, accepting, and nondemanding way. When our clients see the value in trying something that has worked for others we use it as a possible solution and assign it as homework. When our client returns for a follow-up visit and the solution has been a success, we congratulate him for having chosen a solution so wisely. When the homework has been a failure, we simply apologize for leading him astray. We then pick up where we left off and search for exceptions by asking, "When that failed, what did you do that worked better?"

TASKS FOR COUPLES

When we work with couples the logical flow from solution to homework can be complicated by differing views on the value of the solutions. It is normal and expected that couples will view their conflict as caused by their partner. For example, we have often heard the husband complain that his wife nags, while she tells us that he withdraws. Their conflict or dispute can be viewed as two different perspectives colliding with each other. We are often expected to agree with one side or the other. Of course, our experience tells us that agreeing with one side renders us impotent and is not helpful. Since we are more concerned with solutions than explanations or causes of the problem, it is fairly easy to look at their conflicting views as two possible ways to reach the solution, as long as the couple wants the same outcome—to make the relationship work. When you are clear (using scaling questions, for example) that the partners want the same outcome of staying together, you need to validate and support each person's effort as their unique contribution to making the relationship work and find tasks that they both need to do more of.

Even when the couple takes the approach of waiting for the other to change, our task is to help each person pay attention to what the other is doing to be a team. Norm worked with a couple, Eric and Laura, who identified speaking without fear of repercussions as a key to the times they were

Therapist Relationship and Therapeutic Behaviors	
Type of relationship	*Therapeutic behaviors*
Visitor-type relationship	Give frequent positive feedback. Compliment success. Avoid repeating what has not worked. Look for the "hidden customer." Do not give homework.
Customer-type relationship	Compliment on hanging in there. Compliment on commitment, faith, and hope. Capture presession change and deliberate exceptions. Reinforce change with assignments to do more of what works.

able to communicate effectively; each partner was fearful of speaking fearlessly, afraid of what the other might do or say. Since they did have periods when they were able to speak fearlessly, Norm asked them how they did this. Unfortunately, they were unsure about how they achieved these small successes. Norm gave an assignment to each of them: Each was to pick a day to be a "fearless communicator" and not tell the partner which day it was. Because they did not know how they would do this, they had to agree to just do it. It was suggested they try to guess which day their partner picked from observations they would each make while trying to figure out what's different. During the following session Eric was able to guess his wife's "fearless day"; Laura, however, was not able to guess his day of the experiment. It turned out that, not wanting to lose this "game," he had chosen to be fearless everyday. Additionally, by making careful observations of what they did to speak fearlessly to each other, they were able to identify what they had to do to overcome the fear of repercussions.

Quick Tip:

Some Good Words to
Use in Starting
Sentences about
Homework Tasks

*"I agree that it is time to do
something."*

*"Because you have convinced me how serious your
problem is . . ."*

*"Since it is obvious to me
that . . ."*

*"Part of me thinks your kind
of problem calls for action,
while another part of me
thinks you must review this
more."*

ASSIGNING THE HOMEWORK

Homework is our way of extending therapy to the client's natural living environment so that she can practice, experiment, and modify solutions to fit her natural way of living. Homework is designed to remind the client of her preferred future and to do what is good for her. We preface our homework assignments with a message. The message acknowledges our client's view of the problem, validates her opinions about what has gone wrong or right, affirms that she is the expert on how best to proceed with a solution, influences how she has seen her problems and solutions, and offers our view of what might be a first step on the path of change. We use the following guidelines to help us formulate an effective message:

1. Agree with the client. Our customers are always right.

2. Agree with the client's goal. See the wisdom in what she wants.

3. Use the client's language. Keep track of three words the client uses most often and work them into the message.

4. Emphasize that this is a good time to be coming to therapy even though it will take lots of hard work on her part.

5. Offer both direct and indirect compliments. Make note of what the client is doing that is good for her. Also note what the client has already done to proceed toward the goal.

6. Use simple bridging statements for the suggestions you will give. Make sure the rationale for the task you will assign makes sense to the client; use the client's language to express this.

7. All tasks are to help the client feel successful and competent in doing what is good and helpful to her.

8. Offer a simple, easy, doable homework task.

MOST COMMONLY USED HOMEWORK TASKS

1. When there is presession change or clear exceptions to the problem, discuss with the client what it will take to "keep doing" or to "do more" of what already works.

2. When there is a clear behavioral and concrete description of the solution picture (via the miracle question or to prevent the nightmare day), suggest that the client pick a convenient time, day, or place to pretend that the solution actually happened. The emphasis here is on noticing what difference this makes in his life (drinking, marriage, job, etc.), not on doing the homework.

3. When there is small success and few exceptions, and the client is unable to describe how he had these successes, suggest a coin toss experiment so that the client is more conscious of his own successful strategies. Once he is aware of successful steps, it is not difficult to replicate those steps and can increase success.

4. Whatever it is the client is doing that is healthy and helpful and enhances better functioning in her real life, it is worth highlighting and repeating, even when it has no direct bearing on the problem that beings her to therapy. Sometimes, when people try to solve a difficult problem they get stuck in a rut and increasing their effort only deepens the rut. However, as soon as they stop trying to solve the problem (by taking a walk, for instance), a solution literally pops into mind. Clients often report this phenomenon; therefore, we encourage clients to repeat successful behaviors, even when there is no apparent connection between these successful behaviors and the problem.

··

Chapter 5

After the First Session

There is a wonderful, mysterious, and at times unnerving aspect to doing therapy: Therapists, even master therapists, never know how a session went until the follow-up session. Brian Cade, an Australian therapist and coauthor of *A Brief Guide To Brief Therapy*, presented a video of his work with an anorexic young woman. During the final session she compliments Brian on his insight into some dysfunctional family dynamics that helped her see her relationship with her grandmother in a new (and more helpful) light. Yet, there was never any prior mention of family dynamics by either the client or Brian. So, what happened? We don't know exactly, but we do know each of us attributes certain meaning to an event and we all read into things in order to understand them. Clients do the same thing in their own way. Often our lack of understanding is simply our missed opportunity to put the same meaning to an event. The dilemma is, if we don't know how the client is making the therapy work we can't do more of it, and when we can't do more of what works it becomes more difficult to predict success. Though predicting success is not particularly valuable for any one client, it can be important for program planning and the distribution of resources across a clinic's caseload.

To bridge the gap between not knowing if a client will be successful and needing to know if a client needs extra resources to increase the chances for success, Norm tried an experiment with a success prediction scale (see appendix) that clinicians would fill out and score following the first session. The scale was created around the assumption that a client in a customer-type relationship, with workable exceptions to his problem, would be more likely to succeed in therapy than the client who is in a hidden-customer relationship with only a small amount of interest in using therapy to make changes in his life. However, Norm was surprised by his results. When the scores of over 100 client's were compared to their actual success in therapy there was no correlation between a clients initial presentation and positive outcomes. We concluded that using a solution-focused approach helps us know more exactly what a client wants, and puts us in a much better position to be able to help him get it by effectively utilizing *his* resources.

. . . .

Questions from the Field:

Do you think it is important for therapists who work with alcoholics to be in recovery themselves?"

The usual argument put forth in support of the recovering professional involves the matter of relating better to the client and the client's relating better to the therapist. This question of course cannot be answered without first answering a question about self-disclosure. We do not believe that clients come to therapy to hear the therapist's life story. However, clients sometimes are curious about what kind of life their therapist has lived. Before we ever answer a client's question about our personal life we want to know how the information will be helpful. When we discuss what the client needs we seldom, if ever, come to the conclusion that we must disclose our personal life to the client. If the question does persist we prefer to give the information in a matter-of-fact way and return the focus to the client's problems and solutions.

For some clients the matter of relating to people with similar problems is very important. When clients can see people with similar problems living effective lives, it often gives them hope and strength to carry on. When this is an important part of the therapy, we refer clients to AA or one of the recovery support groups in our clinics. We do not believe our clients should have to pay a therapist to get this kind of support when it is freely available in the community or recovery groups.

A WORKABLE SESSION NOTE

Most of the treatment clinics and residential programs we are familiar with still use the ubiquitous SOAP (subjective, objective, assessment, plan) note. Whenever we have spoken with clinicians in the field using solution-focused therapy, inevitably the problem with the SOAP note is discussed (e.g., it is therapist-centered, pathology-oriented). Solution-focused clinicians complain that after a counseling session focused on demythologizing their expert position and pointing the client in a positive and optimistic direction, it is difficult to write a SOAP note. The SOAP format forces them to think in terms of *objective* observations, an expert *assessment*, and a professional prescription in the form of a *plan*. Rather than encourage dedicated clinicians who use our solution-focused ideas to do mental cartwheels, flipping from a competency-based session to a pathology-based session note, we developed a simple solution-focused note that meets the medical record needs of most substance abuse treatment clinics (see appendix).

SECOND AND LATER SESSIONS

Unlike most treatment models, solution-focused therapy emphasizes helping people change rather than eliminating barriers to change. Our focus continues to be on what works and doing more of what works until the client thinks he has attained sufficient progress to stop therapy. The task in second and subsequent sessions is to expand on the small changes the client initiated and motivate them to do even more.

EARS

We have developed some guidelines, organized around the anachronism EARS, to guide therapists through the process of helping problem drinkers recover in second and later sessions. EARS stands for elicit, amplify, reinforce, and start again.

Elicit

Ask about positive change.

1. Open the session by asking, "What's been better?" or "What have you been doing to make your life better?" Do not ask, "Is anything better?" because this tends to elicit a negative answer. During the session explore the relational aspects of change by asking, "What would _____ say is better?"

2. If the client complains, ask, "What was the best day?" or "What was the best part of the day?" Explore exceptions to the problem by asking, "Tell me about the times you were not drinking, even for a short time." Follow up with, "How did you do that?" until you complete the investigation.

3. If the client reports setbacks ask, "What have you learned?" "What has been better this time?" and "What has helped you continue to try?" We have learned that when clients report a setback, something negative usually happened within the preceding 24 hours. When we review the week we often find things were going better just prior to the setback.

• •

Questions from the Field:

"How do you keep solution-focused therapy from being mechanical?"

This is something that seems very difficult for student therapists when they begin using solution-focused therapy. They feel like they are just using the questions they have been given in training or read in a book. Because we have so many questions for the many situations that occur in therapy, it is easy to get confused and think solution-focused therapy is just a bunch of questions and nothing more. This is far from the truth. Solution-focused therapy is not about asking questions; it is about listening to client's answers. When a good therapist listens, the therapy is never mechanical. The sample questions we list here are designed as a guideline. Your individual style will still shine through when using these questions. In fact, we think the traditional therapies that spend many sessions coming up with a DSM-IV diagnosis and then give the client expert advice and a "clinically proven" treatment plan are inhuman and mechanical and do not individualize the treatment.

Tips from the Field:

Changing One Word Can Make a Difference

Replace "Why?" questions with a "How?" or curious "How come?" question; you will instantly become solution-focused. Instead of asking, "Why do you drink?" ask, "You must have some very good reasons for drinking. Can you tell about your good reasons?" Sit back and listen. Then follow with, "Okay, that makes sense. What other good reasons do you have for drinking?" Be prepared to be surprised!

4. If the client reports difficulties ask, "How have you managed?" and "What has been helpful?"

Amplify

Ask for details about positive change.

1. When: "When did this happen?" "Then what happened?" and "Then what happened?"

2. Who: "Who noticed?" "Who else noticed?" "How did they respond?" "When they responded differently, what did you do?" and "What tells you they noticed?"

3. Where: "What was going on there that helped?" "Can you do that same thing elsewhere? Everywhere?"

4. How: "How did you do that?" "How did you know that was the right thing to do?" "How did you (or someone else) decide to do that?" "How did this help?" and "How do you know you can do more of it?"

Reinforce

Make sure the client notices and values positive change.

1. Nonverbal: Lean forward, raise eyebrows, pick up a pen, and take notes.

2. Verbal: Interrupt by asking, "Say that again!" or "You did what?" with an amazed look on your face.

3. Compliment: Compliment the client for what has been done. Even compliment the client for what has not been done by saying, "I'm glad you knew enough to move slowly." Of course, we believe a self-compliment is best, that is, when the client answers your question "How did you do that?" with "I know myself enough to know that I had to eat something before I had my beer."

Start Again

Go back to the beginning and focus on client-generated change.

1. Ask, "What's better since the last time we met?" "How did you do that?" "How did that help?"

2. Ask, "What else did you notice?" "Is that different?" and "How is that helpful?" Also

● ●

Questions from the Field:

"Is there room for spirituality in solution-focused therapy?"

This is a very important question because so much that has been successful in the treatment of clients with drinking problems has been spiritual or what has been called "faith healing." We do not disagree with this approach when it is the approach favored by our client. However, we do not force it on everyone just because it has been a useful concept in some situations. We have listened to many clients who have been turned off by programs that insist they embrace the idea of a higher power or surrender their life and will. Some feminist therapists find this approach particularly harmful to women who are trying to build a self that is free of cultural bondage.

We believe it is spiritual to accept the client's position, here and now, without attempting to force him to change in a certain direction. Respecting a person's dignity, believing in his inherent worth, and acting on that belief is spiritual.

include relational questions like, "What would _____ say he noticed different about you?"

ENDING THERAPY: KNOWING WHEN IT IS GOOD ENOUGH

Traditional therapies tend to view the client-therapist relationship as the vehicle for change. We are aware of many studies that indicate that the relationship a therapist develops with the client is the single most important mechanism of change. We do not disagree with this position; we make every attempt to be warm and friendly with our clients, but our view of the client-therapist relationship is akin to Mary Poppins saying, "A spoonful of sugar helps the medicine go down." The client-therapist relationship encourages the change but does not cause the change. Solution-focused therapy emphasizes clients' seeking their own way of making changes in their life, which we believe is a valuable part of the accepting relationship a therapist and his or her client develops. Thus, we do not use valuable therapeutic time sitting around making friends. Many studies (Howard, Kopta, Kruse, & Orlinski, 1986; Taube, Burns, & Kessler, 1984) indicate that six is the average number of sessions any therapist can expect from a client in an outpatient setting. It is our job to get to work as quickly as possible. Part of that work is deciding when therapy is going to be finished. We begin this job in the first session. A common first-session question is, "How will you know you are finished with therapy?" or "What will you notice (about yourself, about others) that will let you know you do not need to come here anymore?" We also use the scaling question to spark our client's interest in what will be different in a few sessions that will let him know therapy is finished. This approach underlines our belief in helping clients engender a hopeful outlook for themselves. We believe that unless we have absolute hope we cannot inspire hope in others. Clients often come to therapy with the mistaken belief that therapy goes on and on forever and change will be a slow process—which would discourage all of us. By introducing the benchmarks of progress and the endpoint of therapy, we are making a positive statement about our faith

- -

Questions from the Field:

"What do you do when your client shows up drunk?"

When the client is drunk but not too drunk to be passed out somewhere, we assume he is "sober" enough to talk. Although some treatment experts may find talking to an intoxicated client a complete waste of time, we are reminded of the adage, "A drunken mouth speaks from a sober mind." The problem we do, however, encounter with our clients when they come to a session intoxicated is the matter of paying attention. They tend to drift off. We have found two techniques extremely helpful: (1) Insist that both therapist and client stand throughout the session, and (2) go outside for a walk and talk while walking. There is no reason why the "talking cure" should always be done while sitting down, as long as the client can pay attention.

Caution: Under no circumstances should you let your intoxicated client drive away from your office. Arrange for a taxi to take him home. If necessary, call the police.

in our client's ability to build solutions that will make his life better. This faith in the human spirit to heal itself is conveyed throughout our contact in many subtle ways. (And sometimes in not-so-subtle ways. Norm has the word "SOLUTION" printed in 6-inch letters above his office door.)

Frequently, treatment programs decide when to discharge based on the number of sessions that have lapsed or the time put into the program, such as a 12-session group or a 30-day program. We prefer to measure treatment and base decisions about discharge on concrete, behavioral, measurable signs that the client can identify as indicators that her recovery is moving in the right direction. The client's confidence that she can stay at a 7 or 8 for a considerable period of time generally seems to be a good guideline.

WHAT ABOUT RELAPSE?

Contrary to most therapists' views, it seems that clients return to treatment after they have stopped drinking (again), not in the middle of a relapse. The client is on the way back up to the previous level of functioning. In the medical model of addiction, relapse means the client must start over from scratch. In programs like AA, when a member relapses he must refigure his sobriety date and start counting the sober days over with day one. We disagree with this view. Relapse is a normal learning experience. Relapse means that there was a success: Without successful abstinence there would be no relapse. Most relapse prevention programs we are familiar with focus on what happened just before the relapse occurred, on what triggered the relapse, such as how upset she was, what he forgot to do, how he was hungry, lonely, tired, and angry, without doing anything about it. We focus our attention on different areas.

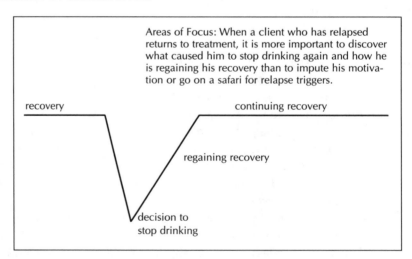

Areas of Focus: When a client who has relapsed returns to treatment, it is more important to discover what caused him to stop drinking again and how he is regaining his recovery than to impute his motivation or go on a safari for relapse triggers.

recovery continuing recovery

regaining recovery

decision to
stop drinking

1. What happened just before the relapse ended? "How did you know it was time to stop drinking again?" It is vital to get a rich description of this "getting ready to stop again" solution-moment by asking for a detailed account, for instance, "What was telling you it was time to stop?" "When did

you notice your plan to drink again was not working?" "When did you realize you wanted to stop again?" "Where were you when you wanted to stop drinking?" "Who, besides yourself, was instrumental in making this decision?" and "How did you go about getting to the point of stopping again?"

2. We want to know the details of how the client stayed sober before the relapse. In our view, the client's previous recovery has not been sullied by this relapse. Prepare yourself to hear as rich a description of the client's previous recovery as is possible.

3. How is the client staying sober now? With very few exceptions, clients return to treatment *after* they have either made the decision to stop drinking or have already stopped drinking. It is safe to assume this has been accomplished with a great deal of effort. Knowing about this effort will be helpful in developing strategies for further recovery.

4. What is different about this relapse and staying sober, compared to previous ones? We are very curious about the details of how he gets himself back on the right track, especially when he has been able to do this before.

There are many instances when our client has returned to therapy following a relapse with the idea that this time treatment was going to take a very long time. However, when we had answers to the above questions, we were both satisfied that a single session of therapy was all that was needed to rebuild a workable solution. Most clients simply need a reminder of what they already know how to do.

WHEN TO REFER TO A MORE (OR LESS) INTENSIVE LEVEL OF CARE

Our clients are valuable resources to our therapy programs. They bring a variety of solutions to our groups, making for an exciting mix of strategies for change. We want to keep them. When working in a managed care outpatient setting, there is pressure to see clients in the least restrictive and least costly modality that is clinically possible. These factors, as well as our clinical concerns, are part of a decision-making process about the appropriate level of care. The only factor that must override them is the efficacy of service at any given level of care. We must do what is best for our clients. Rather than reinvent the wheel, we support the use of the ASAM (American Society of Addiction Medicine, Inc.) Patient Placement Criteria for Substance-Related Disorders (1996). Though pathological in orientation, the ASAM criteria have become commonplace in the United States, making their use almost mandatory by even the most ardent solution-focused therapist. The ASAM criteria assist clinicians in making clinically appropriate referrals by describing levels of care ranging from outpatient services through hospitalization and referencing each level of care with six dimensions, each of which contains key placement criteria that a patient must meet. These criteria, however, in no way prepare a client or a facility for the work ahead. Clients often arrive at a treatment center with no idea of what is expected of them. Family members can also remain in the dark, not knowing what is expected of them and how they should behave toward their loved one when he returns. So, when making a referral, we have the client and his family, answer the following questions. We then fax the answers to the staff at the other end of the referral.

1. What is the goal of treatment? What will be different when you are discharged that will let you know we are making the right decision?

2. What are the benchmarks that will let you know you are continuing to move in the right direction? How will your friends and family know you are making progress?

3. What previous experiences do you have that will help make this expenditure of time and money worthwhile? How will you put these experiences into action? How will you know your experience is paying off?

4. What needs to be different when you return to maximize your success? How will this happen? Who do you need to ask for help? What would be helpful for them to start now?

• •

Questions from the Field:

"What about clients who are in denial?"

We believe denial is in the eye of the beholder. The word denial is used to describe the client when he disagrees with the professional and they do not see things the same way. We have found that describing a client as "in denial" is not a very useful concept. When someone is in denial the natural tendency for the therapist is to shake the client up and show him the truth, thus attempting to break through the denial. This usually takes the shape of confrontation, which usually means that the therapist points out the misguided view of the client. In other words, we are right and he is wrong.

We believe it is not affirming or empowering to point out anyone's misguided notions. It is embarrassing and humiliating to have your face rubbed in the consequences of your drinking. It is always better when the client decides that his viewpoint is no longer working and that he needs to do something different. We believe this is not only much more respectful and empowering, but also recovery is faster because the solution belongs to him, not the professional.

•••

Chapter 6

How It All Fits Together:
A Case Study

This is a condensed account of three sessions that took place in the summer of 1994. The sessions were held in the clinic of a health maintenance organization. Norm was the therapist and he was helped by a team who viewed the session on closed circuit television.

John (the client) is a 34-year-old skilled carpenter who presented with problems of substance abuse, grief, trust, and an undisclosed problem referred to in this manuscript as "problem B." During an intake interview, conducted over the telephone, John informed the clinician that he had been seen there (in the same HMO clinic) for marriage therapy and urged that the therapist he would be working with read his case history so that he would not have to repeat that information. The clinician collecting the intake information assured John that Norm would read the case history. Because of this promise Norm did familiarize himself with the previous therapist's detailed notes, although he does not usually do this, preferring to meet the client "fresh." You will notice that Norm concentrates on the client's current concerns, not the historical material, during this interview.

SESSION I
Establishing a Goal

NORM: So . . . you came here today to talk about something. What can I do that will be helpful for you?

JOHN: I really don't know. I don't know where to start. I smoke pot every-day.

NORM: Is that one of the things you've come to talk about today?

JOHN: Um, sure. I don't know where this is going to lead. Um, I don't know if I have a problem with, I mean, smoking pot. I mean, it's not like—I'm not doing cocaine, I'm not doing heroin, I don't shoot. I guess sometimes it's become a financial liability.

NORM: Yeah, it can get that way after a while.

JOHN: No. No. I mean, not on a severe scale. I guess, I mean, how do people look at how much pot, I mean, do you look at it dollarwise or how much you consume?

NORM: Yeah.

JOHN: I mean, I don't know. I mean, is it good or bad?

NORM: However you want to . . .

JOHN: I mean, is it good or bad for me?

NORM: What do you think?

JOHN: Getting up in the morning is bad for you too. I think the only reason it's bad for me is because it's given me a respiratory problem, but I'm not smoking cigarettes. I've just been doing it for so long, it's like, you know, why give it up now?

NORM: Okay. What does your wife say? Does she think it's a problem?

JOHN: Yes and no. Yes it's a problem when we don't have money and if I go buy some; no it's not a problem if it's limited use.

NORM: You're a little iffy on it, she's a little iffy on it.

JOHN: I don't know if I smoke pot as a shield maybe. You get high and you don't have to deal with the reality of something.

NORM: Then pot helps you somehow . . .

JOHN: Oh, I get up at 5 in the morning and I smoke by 5:30.

NORM: Mmhmm.

JOHN: I mean it's . . . I've been doing that for 10 years.

NORM: And how does it help you if you do that?

JOHN: Oh, it's just like a cigarette smoker gets up and before he goes to the bathroom he smokes a cigarette in the morning. At least I give myself, you know, a little bit more time.

NORM: So, mostly for cigarette smokers, that's to get the nicotine going in their system to prevent them from getting real shaky and irritable.

JOHN: Well, I mean, I mean, some people if they don't smoke pot they get shaky and irritable.

NORM: Do you?

JOHN: No, I don't get shaky, I get irritable.

NORM: You get irritable though.

JOHN: Yeah.

NORM: Okay. So then if you smoke pot, then you don't get irritable.

JOHN: That's true. (Pause) I'm not a junkie. At least I hope I'm not, you know. There's a bunch of other things. I think I've used pot previously to hide things, you know, um, I've had some friends who've died, my brother died a year ago . . .

NORM: I'm sorry.

JOHN: I've been incarcerated for a while. I guess I've come to some times in life when it really sucks. I've had the opportunity where, why even be here?

But I'm still here. Why give up? You know, there must be something in store for me. I mean, I don't know, I don't drink often, I just smoke a lot of pot. And I'm not hurting anyone but myself . . . I mean, I'm on parole . . . um, but, that's no big deal to them because my embezzlement isn't drug-or alcohol-related, and they know that if I'm left alone, then everything's hunky-dory.

Within just a few minutes of conversation notice how much information the client volunteers about his difficulties with the use of pot. The more patient Norm is, the more the client comes to his conclusion that his pot use is creating problems for him.

NORM: Okay. So you've got the pot thing. Is there anything else we should be discussing?

JOHN: The other problem can be a legal setback, I guess. Financial . . . it has become a semifinancial setback.

NORM: Okay, so it's definitely a financial . . .

JOHN: Well, it's cost me almost $2000.

NORM: Oh.

JOHN: Right. I mean you pay 60 bucks for your pot. It takes 60 bucks a week for the other problem because I've broken it down into a payment plan. I have another $56 that's expected to come out of my check for health insurance for us, so I mean I have to start . . . weigh some options here.

NORM: Okay. What kind of work do you do?

JOHN: I build custom homes.

NORM: Oh.

JOHN: In the $300,000- and $400,000-and-up range.

NORM: Are you good at it?

JOHN: Yeah. So I don't know where to go, what to do. I guess I could be like my best friend, Paul. I could, you know, commit suicide and forget it all, but you know, I have my son, Sam, and my wife, Sandy, and why do I want to lose that?

His problems are clearly overwhelming to the client and can easily become the same for the therapist, especially the talk of suicide. Instead of becoming alarmed by his talk of suicide, we suggest at this point that you keep in mind that the client is seeking help and is clearly distressed about his dilemma. Now that Norm has a broad view of John's difficulties, it is time to discuss the detailed picture of John's view of solutions to his very serious problems.

The Miracle Question

NORM: (Pause) Okay, well . . . let me think for a moment. Okay, I have an odd question. If you go home today, you go about your business. You go back to work, it comes this evening, you fall asleep, and in the middle of the night a miracle occurs, and all of the problems that you've brought here today are suddenly (snaps fingers) gone . . . they are not problems anymore, but because this miracle occurs in the middle of the night you don't know about it. What would be the first thing that you would notice that would let you know that this miracle has taken place?

JOHN: I wouldn't hack up half a lung in the morning, every morning.

NORM: So you'd wake up and you wouldn't be coughing?

JOHN: I wouldn't be coughing. I have a real bad stomach too. So, I've traumatized my body since I was probably about 10.

NORM: So in the absence of the hacking, what would be taking place as you woke up?

JOHN: I'd be getting to work quicker. I'd get up, I go to the bathroom, I cough, I go to work.

NORM: Mmhmm.

JOHN: Sometimes I throw food into my lunchbox, otherwise I buy, I eat a lot of grease and uh . . .

NORM: Okay.

JOHN: Hamburgers.

NORM: So on this miracle day, how would you be starting the day that would let you know that . . .

It is common for the client to regress to problem talk (Furman & Ahola, 1992). Notice how Norm gently steers the conversation to solution talk. The more detailed the solution description, the better it is. Also notice how Norm uses the client's exact words to formulate the next question.

JOHN: Very placid. I wouldn't be hacking, I'd be to work, I'd be fresh, I'd be crisp.

NORM: (Pause) And how would that help you? On that day, how would that help you to be waking up placid and crisp and fresh?

JOHN: Probably be . . . I don't know if I want to say focused, because I'm always focused at work . . . um . . . (long pause) I'd just be in a better frame of mind.

NORM: What would you call that frame of mind? What label would you put on it?

JOHN: (Pause) I can't think of what I'd put on it. I'd just be a . . . I probably wouldn't be in an obnoxious mood. I get to work, we're all obnoxious.

NORM: It would not be obnoxious at least.

JOHN: Right.

NORM: And what would your wife notice about your frame of mind?

JOHN: She wouldn't notice anything, she's still sleeping.

NORM: She's still sleeping?

JOHN: Oh yeah, she sleeps.

NORM: Oh. When would she notice the miracle had occurred?

JOHN: Probably when she got home.

NORM: That would be like late afternoon?

JOHN: Yeah, it'd be late afternoon.

NORM: She's got a day job too?

JOHN: Yeah, I probably wouldn't be cranky or something. (Pause) It takes me an hour to wind down after work. You know, you have such an adrenaline flow . . .

NORM: So on the miracle day, what would she notice?

JOHN: I probably wouldn't be as cranky. My normal routine when I get home, I just don't get home and change and shower. I usually get home and sweep, put the dishes away, wash the previous dishes, pick up the house. She'd probably just notice that I wasn't cranky or something, or I might go for a walk or bike ride with them.

NORM: Um . . .

JOHN: I mean, you work hard all day long, you know, your body's tired. At night I really don't feel like going for a bike ride or walk. You know, usually my right knee will hurt after work, and my right hand, so . . . my right hand's been wrecked and my right knee is almost shot.

NORM: Okay. So it might not be the bike ride, but you might go for a walk.

JOHN: Right, I might go for a walk or do something that—

NORM: You mean just with your wife, just the two of you?

JOHN: The three of us.

NORM: The three of you?

JOHN: Yeah.

NORM: What would your son notice on this miracle day?

JOHN: I'd probably buy him something.

NORM: Oh.

JOHN: So that would really turn him on.

NORM: What would you buy him?

JOHN: Uh, something that he wants. He's a gimme, gimme, gimme type. He's 6, so he wants, I don't know, he probably wants some sort of Power Ranger thing. We have so many Power Rangers, GI Joes, Ninja Turtles, Play Mobiles . . . he has it all. You name it, we got it. Toys.

NORM: And on this miracle day you might buy him something more. You might take a walk with your family. Well you've got my curiosity, what else?

JOHN: I might wash my hair.

NORM: Oh. You might wash your hair. Before or after the walk?

JOHN: When I'm taking a shower. Sorry, that's my deal this summer, not washing my hair.

NORM: How would these things help you?

JOHN: I'd probably feel better . . . I'd probably feel a lot better. You know, I mean, I'm 30 years old. Of course I've noticed things from smoking pot and drinking heavily and, you know, drinking, drugging, working hard. You know, I mean, I get headaches you know, and I mean, around 9 o'clock I go to bed, and you notice those things. It's like . . . but it's fun and nice to be high . . . to get high, you know? I mean, I don't know if you know.

NORM: Well, let me ask you, on this miracle day, um . . . and you're not getting high, and the other problem isn't there, um . . . what would you be doing to make sure that you didn't do those things on this miracle day?

JOHN: I wouldn't have to do anything. The miracle would have happened. They're gone. They're not a thought . . . they're out of my thought pattern.

NORM: Oh, so they'd be completely out of your thought pattern?

JOHN: Well, it's a miracle day.

NORM: Right.

JOHN: (Pause) I mean, getting high, I've come to like it and it's fun, it's enjoyable, it's relaxing, it takes the tension off. You can be real flustered at work. You can't figure out a rafter pattern or something, three or four of you can twist out the number (smoke a joint of pot), you relax, you stop yelling at each other and take the calculator back out and push the numbers in the right way . . .

NORM: Mmhmm.

JOHN: The other problem, the other problem (yawning) . . . that would be nice to be gone, but I think it's a problem that has come from, I don't know where it's come from.

Contextualizing the Miracle Day to Fit the Client's Goals

NORM: Well, then let's take this . . . let's take this placidness, this crispness, this focus, this family activity, let's take it all and let's carry it into a day with another miracle, but not quite so miraculous. Let's make the second miracle day a day when you have thoughts of doing these things that you've come here—

JOHN: It would be like today. It would be normal.

NORM: But on this miracle day you don't . . . you don't use. You don't do whatever the other problem is. What would you notice about yourself on that day?

JOHN: So I wouldn't get high?

NORM: You wouldn't get high.

JOHN: And problem #2 wouldn't come up?

NORM: And problem #2 wouldn't come up.

JOHN: What would be different?

NORM: What would you notice is different about yourself on that kind of miracle day?

JOHN: It'd just be a normal, boring day (laughs).

NORM: A normal, boring day?

JOHN: There's got to be some excitement in every day. I mean, it would be nice to get up, you know, I mean, that's exciting. I mean, I like getting up and—

NORM: When's the last time you had a normal, boring day?

JOHN: Yesterday, I mean Sunday. Sunday is usually the worst day of the week for me. I'm usually in a real bad mood all day Sunday. Got up at 5 o'clock, drove to Maine, played in the sun all day.

NORM: No drugs?

JOHN: Oh yeah. We dealt with that though. Didn't drink though.

NORM: Didn't drink? Had a little pot . . .

JOHN: Oh yeah. Not too much. Had to drive.

NORM: Okay. What did you do to limit your use?

JOHN: I was driving. Had to concentrate. Had to make sure everybody got there safely and got home safely (yawns).

NORM: You were with your wife and Sam?

JOHN: Yup. And we had some friends who were following us in their car.

NORM: So safety is something you're concerned about?

JOHN: Oh yeah. Oh definitely.

NORM: Don't want to see your family hurt?

JOHN: I'm very cautious, I'm aware of my surroundings and what's going on . . . and, I mean, that comes from being incarcerated. You know, I've seen too much hurt . . .

NORM: So . . .

JOHN: Too much hurt in 30 years and too much death to see any more.

NORM: So . . . back to this smaller miracle day. On this smaller miracle day, when you completely refrain from using drugs and refrain from this other problem, what would you notice you had to do to pull that off? To actually get through the without using?

JOHN: I don't . . . I mean if I ran out of pot, I mean I wait 'til Friday. You know, I get paid on Friday. So if I run out tomorrow, tomorrow's Tuesday, Wednesday, Thursday, Friday . . .

NORM: You would need a couple of miracle days in there.

JOHN: Oh yeah. I mean, um . . . you know, everybody at work smokes pot, so if, you know, if one guy runs out, you know, you still catch a buzz during the day.

NORM: Yeah.

JOHN: But, I mean, I usually don't get high at night. We just get high during the day at work (yawns).

NORM: How do you do that?

JOHN: How do I do what?

NORM: Not get high at night? How do you do that?

JOHN: Too tired.

NORM: Just too tired?

JOHN: Come home, shower, do something, have dinner, do the dishes, put Sam to bed.

NORM: How does being too tired help you not do pot?

JOHN: It doesn't. I just don't have the energy to do it. I mean, point A, I'm tired. If I get high in between point B, you know . . . you know, it's a waste. I'd be wasting money. Look at it that way.

NORM: Okay, and that is a consequence you are concerned about.

JOHN: Oh yeah.

NORM: In both of these problems, you've got a waste of money.

JOHN: Well, I mean . . . I betcha an alcoholic spends more than $50, $60 a week drinking. I don't drink that much because I've seen what it does to a good friend of mine who's now dead . . . too many friends of mine, so I mean, I drank heavily when I was in junior high school and the early years of high school, and my body can't take alcohol that heavily anymore. I mean, I was at a Grateful Dead concert (two weeks before this interview) and I drank a liter of Captain Morgan—

NORM: Mmhmm.

JOHN: —and it took me two days to recover from that just about. I mean, I went to work, but I was just barely moving. The next day I didn't get up 'til 8 o'clock. Got five hours of sleep and then went to work . . . everybody was hung over (laughs).

NORM: You just reminisced about the concert?

JOHN: Yeah, we sure did.

Asking for a Working Session Goal

NORM: Okay . . . well, what would be different about your life as a result of this meeting that would let you know that this was worth coming here?

JOHN: Say that again? What would be worth it?

NORM: Yeah. What would be different about your life as a result of coming here today that would tell you, "Hey, that was worth it"?

JOHN: Nothing's going to tell me today.

NORM: Nothing?

JOHN: I don't think it's something for myself that is gonna happen overnight.

NORM: Okay . . . let's spread it out then, a couple of sessions. Make it more general. What would make it worthwhile for you to come to counseling?

JOHN: I don't know, you know, I mean, I don't know why I've been smoking pot since I was 14. I don't know why I started drinking when I was 11. (Pause) Well, I don't think I'm sick. I might be wacked a little bit, but, um . . . you know, where do I go from here? What steps can I take to make myself healthier through food and function? How I can make my mental health stable? What can keep me from getting angry? What can help me deal with problem B, and what can help me deal with my brother's death, why my best friend is dead, why a good friend of mine is dying (laughs), and how do I deal with all this death, because I'll tell ya, it really gets to me.

NORM: Yeah, yeah.

JOHN: And uh . . . big time.

NORM: Yeah, that would be very hard.

JOHN: Yup. The death part's pretty hard to deal with.

NORM: That would be the first thing?

JOHN: Probably.

NORM: Probably?

JOHN: Because, I've got the answer, I know I do (tearful, hesitant voice). I'm so bummed out, I'm mad.

NORM: Mmhmm.

JOHN: That's it.

NORM: And the answer you say you've got?

JOHN: That's it. That's the answer. That's my answer. That's what's wrong with me. I'm so bummed out, I'm mad.

NORM: (Pause) You don't want to be mad anymore?

JOHN: No, not really. Life's been kind of hard. I'd like it to get easy.

Notice how Norm is leading and following John at the same time, leading toward realistic, workable solutions that John generates and following him by using his words, successes, and ideas for success. The details of successful strategies that the client describes are generated by the client.

Search for Exceptions

NORM: Oh yeah. No doubt about it. So, let me start almost all over again. Has there been any day since all these various people have died when you haven't been angry . . . when there's been something else going on?

JOHN: Oh yeah. Most definitely.

NORM: And what was that day like?

JOHN: You know, I've done other things, like I haven't gotten high and stuff like that. I mean, I'm not saying that it's great, I mean, it's wonderful.

NORM: And some of those days you're a little bit less angry? Did more of something else?

JOHN: No . . . I'm . . . there are days when there's no drugs or anything. I mean, I can get cranky, but, I mean, I can control myself, I can. I mean, you obviously know if you're in a situation that you can't get angry, you just keep it in . . . you just . . . put on a happy face, and just stay happy. You know, you make a comment, "Well that was pretty asinine what so-and-so did, you know, that kinda irritated me a little bit," so I mean I might go over and say, "Sorry Mr. Smith, but I think that was pretty stupid and it upset me that you did that."

NORM: Yeah.

JOHN: I mean, there are people I know who would do that and I think it embarrasses themselves, but . . .

NORM: So, how do you control it?

JOHN: I just . . . I just walk away, I mean, I'll walk away from someone rather than getting loud or obnoxious and making a comment to them.

NORM: And how does that help you deal with this grief you carry with you?

JOHN: Um . . . well, for the situation it helps. I was incarcerated for two weeks and my best friend of 20 years committed suicide. I had another friend wreck his motorcycle and get killed, another real good friend who I grew up with is dying of AIDS, my brother died, a very good friend moved last September just before my brother died, to North Carolina and, it's just one thing after another . . .

NORM: Yeah.

JOHN: But life goes on.

Creating a Scale

NORM: Let me ask you something here that may be very difficult. To put your grief on a scale of 1 to 10, and 1 is it at its most intense, it is as painful as it's been, and 10 is you resolved it, you're able to go on in your life, what would you say you are?

JOHN: Probably a 6. I guess time heals everything.

NORM: I was going to ask you, for you, what's the difference between 1 and 6?

JOHN: Time.

NORM: And what have you done with that time to . . .

JOHN: Go to work, go to work.

NORM: And how does work help?

JOHN: I have to concentrate on work. When I go to work I even forget about the family. I can't function in the team if I'm thinking about something else. You know, my brother died on a Friday, we buried him on Tuesday, and I was at work on Wednesday. I went back to work.

NORM: Okay. And it helps the overall process of grief?

JOHN: Yeah, I mean, yeah. I get up, I leave for work and, you know, I'm married but I'm not thinking about them. I'm thinking about work. I get to talking to the guys at work and I'm thinking about what do I need? Where am I setting up? Who's working with me? I'm at work.

NORM: Okay. So, time and work helped you go from 1 to 6. Anything else help you go from 1 to 6?

JOHN: Probably getting high a little bit.

NORM: (Pause) And I take it that your goal, one of the things that you will be saying, "Okay counseling is worth it," is if you can go from 6 to 10?

JOHN: Yeah.

NORM: Okay, anything else? (Pause) I'm going to take a break and talk to the team.

JOHN: Where do we go? You know, what do I do on my end?

NORM: Okay. That's a good question you've asked a couple of times. Okay. You can wait in here if you want, or you can wait out in the waiting room.

JOHN: Okay.

Now that the conversation has generated a great deal of information on John's pain, aspirations, and his dilemma, it is time to put a closure on the session by summarizing the conversation. The compliments highlight what the client has described as the desired outcome and his hidden strengths and resources that will help him reach his goal. The following are typical messages and suggestions given at the conclusion of a first session.

Compliments and Homework

JOHN: (Pointing to *DSM III-R* book) I looked myself up. I'm 305.20.

NORM: Okay.

JOHN: So you'll look in the book on that?

NORM: Oh I trust you. Well, there are some things that I noticed throughout the session. The first thing is your concern for your family responsibility and your work responsibility. That's good. You can be proud of that. It showed up in a couple of places. You referred to the other people at work as a team.

JOHN: Umhmm.

NORM: That indicates a pretty high level of responsibility that you feel toward your coworkers. You talked about being able to refrain from using chemicals too much—

JOHN: Umhmm.

NORM: —while driving. Your concern about safety. You are trying to limit your use of marijuana, eventually maybe even stop using that all together. Trying to address this other problem in some way that's creative so that it's not recurring. I was also impressed with your ability to feel . . . particularly in how you talk about grief. The feelings come up, they are right there on the surface, and that's something that is obvious, that your grief has been hard, it's touched me . . . I want to say, "Okay, here's a guy who's honest."

JOHN: My only comment to that is, it's taken a long time to get to that point. To be honest with you or myself about how I feel.

NORM: Okay. So, now you want to do something. I want you to do something too, something that will add to the work you've already begun. I would like you to continue to be an honest and attentive observer of yourself. I want you to notice what helps you move your grief from a 6 to about a 6½. And to come back and tell about that.

JOHN: Sure. Oh yeah.

NORM: What is it that will move your grief from 6 to 6½? Then, if you've already begun some of that, to a 7, and that's where we'll start next time. Okay?

JOHN: Sure.

[End of session 1]

SESSION 2

The second and later sessions usually begin with asking about what has been better since the last meeting. Notice how the question is phrased with the positive and optimistic expectation that something is better, rather than, "Is something better?"

Search for Progress

NORM: What's better with your life?

JOHN: How about what's worse?

NORM: Well . . .

JOHN: My truck is dead or dying.

NORM: Okay.

JOHN: I need it for the job.

NORM: So, nothing's better?

JOHN: Let's see, what's better? What would be better? Oh, we had a good weekend, Sandy and I. We had a great weekend. I think that was the best thing for us this week. We went out.

NORM: Who put that together? Did you put that together, or did someone else?

JOHN: Sandy did. She let me go out Friday night and play poker.

NORM: How did that help?

JOHN: Going out Friday night?

NORM: Going out Friday night and the poker game.

JOHN: Well, it gave us some space, you know, like we were going out Saturday night and she said if I wanted to go out Friday night it would be all right. It's probably not, as long as I was out, she probably wanted me home earlier.

NORM: And the space alone and the space together helped you to . . .

JOHN: We did our usual family stuff, which is always good. Besides going to work every day.

NORM: And, how does having that kind of week and weekend, how does that help you?

JOHN: I guess it helps good and bad.

Creating a Scale

NORM: Okay. Let me ask you this kind of assessment question. Um . . . scales. We did some scales last time, 1 to 10. 1 being the long list of the problems are at their worst and 10 is a time when those problems are behind you, what would you give this week?

JOHN: Probably a 5. I think this was a 5.

NORM: And . . .

JOHN: The reason being, you know, my truck this morning. That's what really bummed me out you know . . . you build a house and you got to be with it.

NORM: Okay.

JOHN: You're part of it, you become part of it, you know, because if you like—

NORM: And that's higher than a 5?

JOHN: Yeah. That's when things are going good, you know, you're into it, you know, when things go really well and the cog is smooth, then it's smooth at home, and you know, if you have a rough day at work it trickles down.

NORM: Okay. You're pretty smooth right now?

JOHN: Um yeah. I think I'm going to be very gung-ho as soon as I get out of work today because I have something to take care of.

Defining a Goal

NORM: What do you want to see as a result of today's session?

JOHN: Well, I could have been at work, all bent out of shape. You know, this way I guess I stayed at a 5 instead of going lower. (Gestures with a hand) I'm more this than going like this. You know. I'm less manic.

NORM: Okay. So, "worth it" would be just to stabilize you. Okay.

JOHN: So that we could start stepping into things a little bit deeper and go ahead and start developing some ways to stop smoking and drinking.

NORM: What has to happen?

JOHN: Trust. If I can't trust you, then, I mean, what's the use?

NORM: Okay. And how will you know you trust me?

JOHN: You can feel it. You just know that you trust people. I mean I don't—

NORM: So, do you feel this now?

JOHN: Yeah. If I, I mean, if you're not here next week, if I don't trust you I'm gonna get the hell out. You know, I feel comfortable so far. I got pretty well inebriated this weekend. Got a ride by (the campus) police.

NORM: Oh, I didn't—

JOHN: But, but, I was glad about that. I wasn't driving. He gave me a ride home.

NORM: Yep, you mentioned that.

JOHN: Staggering drunk. I had to get a ride there in the morning to fetch the car with Sandy, but—

NORM: So, would you like to do that today? Get some feedback on how to stop smoking pot and drinking?

JOHN: I don't need to get feedback today, but continuously, you know, talked about that stuff. I don't know if it's an evaluation or whatever, but I looked at the book in your office. Marijuana abuse.

NORM: So do you think about your marijuana use differently?

JOHN: Um, well, yes and no, I guess. I wouldn't pass a urine test ever in my life. Probably from age 14 until now. Even when I was incarcerated I was out all day long, I wasn't in jail, so I mean, I was in contact with the public and you saw people that you knew, and one hand washes the other.

NORM: So, do you think that at some point you can change smoking and drinking?

JOHN: Well, I'll probably, I don't know if I'll try to always drink. I've stopped smoking, I've stopped drinking . . .

Looking Into the Future

NORM: What are your options? Have you ever thought about that? What are the various paths you can go down?

JOHN: Well, I could lose my memory, my mind, my—

NORM: Yeah, if you keep smoking large amounts okay, so that's one option. Option #1 is just to—

JOHN: Healthwise—

NORM: Keep smoking and drinking. What are your other options?

JOHN: Stopping.

NORM: Stopping?

JOHN: I mean I don't sell it, so I don't have to worry about, you know, going to jail over it.

NORM: Okay.

JOHN: I mean that's the least of my problems.

NORM: The other options are keep on just doing what you're doing, stop marijuana, stop alcohol, or stop both. I guess there are a bunch of options.

JOHN: All of the above. I mean, I don't know. I work with people who don't smoke. I work with a lot of people who do smoke. One guy drinks all day long, counterproductive. At work I still move right along.

NORM: What would be different about your life when you didn't drink and smoke?

JOHN: Healthwise it would probably be different. As far as I know it would be different. I mean we talked about that last week. I came here last Monday, right?

NORM: Yeah.

JOHN: Tuesday was pretty hard hit. I didn't get high until about 4 in the afternoon. So, I mean, usually—

NORM: Wow.

JOHN: So—

NORM: How did you do that?

JOHN: Concentrate, I guess.

NORM: Concentrate?

JOHN: You know I did work, work, work, that day, all day long. No one at work could believe it. A working dog.

NORM: How did you get through to 4:00? You say you usually start in the morning.

JOHN: Usually, but I didn't.

NORM: So what did you do instead?

JOHN: Went right to work, read the paper real quick and had a donut and went right to work. I didn't do anything until it was time to quit. It wasn't too bad. I mean, I, no one noticed anything different . . . they just say, "No big thing."

NORM: Did you notice anything different?

JOHN: Um, maybe my concentration was a little deeper. Maybe I was a little more productive. Maybe I was more thoughtful of what I was doing.

NORM: Okay, you've got basically three options: Keep smoking and drinking, stop smoking and drinking, or do somehow a combination of keeping some, stopping others.

JOHN: Yeah, but then I'd stop and they'd legalize marijuana.

NORM: There are risks; change involves risks.

JOHN: Yeah.

NORM: Okay, well, which one would you pick? Which one would you pick for yourself?

JOHN: Well, see, I mean, I don't know, I'd have to evaluate the same as now, nothing changed, everything changes. Sandy and I, I mean, everybody. I mean, we don't fight, I mean, everyday, and scream and yell. We just scream and yell for a few minutes.

NORM: Which one would you pick?

JOHN: Um, I'd probably pick the stop both.

Creating a Scale

NORM: (Pause) And now you're somewhere between 1 and 10 on "want to stop them both"—where are you?

JOHN: 5.

NORM: You're at a 5?

JOHN: Maybe at a 4, but I'd say a 5, progressing.

NORM: So at the worst, you're at a 4 progressing to 5?

JOHN: Going up, I keep thinking 1 is lowest.

NORM: Well, on this scale a 10 would mean you'd stopped?

JOHN: Right. I don't mean, you know, I mean, I'm just up to, I'm too in between, you know.

NORM: What I want to know is, what is different at a 7? You're at a 5 now, a 4 now, you're headed in that direction . . .

JOHN: Probably I would see, I would see the, the steps of limitation, and being happier and maybe being in the detox stage, not having the bitchiness, I'd be getting through it.

NORM: You'd be getting through it. Getting through the detox?

JOHN: Yeah.

NORM: Through the bitchiness?

JOHN: Yeah. Yeah. I mean, I used to be able, if I didn't get high, I mean, I used to be in a position with a company I worked for, if I didn't get high, I mean someone would get me high or they knew I was gonna be on them all day.

NORM: Umhmm.

JOHN: I mean, they knew it was hell. Whew, bad.

NORM: So you got other people believing that you've got to get high?

JOHN: Well, we all believe it at work, but I'm sure I would feel a lot better physically and mentally if I started to stop smoking pot.

NORM: So you think you would feel better?

JOHN: I mean, I've spent time as straight as I can be. I mean, I've spent summers at camp where it's just not available. You're out in the middle of the ocean and there's no way, there's no boat comes by and can sell you a dime bag so you can twist it up. I mean, there's nothing. I mean, you get there, they go through your stuff and you're a boot licker when they find your joint. That I know.

NORM: So, how did you do it then?

JOHN: I was just active. I mean, I was climbing cliffs and sailing boats off in the middle of the Atlantic. I mean, I wasn't sitting at home at night and watching Dan Rather and twisting up a doobie, catching the news, seeing all these people getting killed, and you know, all the stupid, mindless stuff that doesn't really need to be happening. I don't want to get bored.

NORM: So what do you do at 6?

JOHN: What do I do at 6? I don't watch channel 5.

Norm: No, no, not at 6 P.M. What do you do at a number 6?

JOHN: Um . . .

NORM: If your idea of 7 is realizing the steps?

JOHN: 6 would be the start. 6 would be like last week; Tuesday was probably progressing to a 6. That was like today. I could go on forever if you've got the afternoon. I mean, we can keep going, I don't have to get back to work.

Do More of What Works

NORM: How many "Tuesdays" do you want next week?

JOHN: Um, well I'm sure I'm gonna try to do the same thing tomorrow. I go home, see, if I go home, and say, well (smacks hands) Sandy, I'm not, like I did this last week, I'm not gonna smoke any pot tomorrow. I'm gonna try as hard as I can. I've left it at home, did come home you know, I live a half-mile away from the house so, I mean, I can go home if I want to get it, you know, I left it at home, I, you know.

NORM: So tomorrow?

JOHN: That's not something I do, trust me I don't leave it at home, and I did and, you know, it didn't bother me. I mean, you know, I just la-di-da'd right through the day and we finished up the day and Frank was drinking some beers and someone pulled out a pipe, filled it up, and I was like, well, it's the end of the day . . .

NORM: So you are thinking about, maybe, tomorrow?

JOHN: Oh yeah, I'm down at this other house.

NORM: And you'd probably tell Sandy?

JOHN: I'm with some very square people down there, I mean, so . . .

NORM: Okay.

JOHN: Trust me. One is leaving Wednesday to become a game warden. He promises to come back and bust us all.

NORM: Oh.

JOHN: And the other one is so square that he's red. He's a big hick. Sorry.

NORM: That's okay. It there anything else I should know about today?

JOHN: I've been dealing with counselors for quite some time.I mean, the first person I ever saw was Don. He was up in John Dewey Hall. He kinda kicked back and like, what are you drinking for, and I was in high school and drinking already. I went, yeah, I drank before I got here too, you know. And he was like, see you next week. And I just expected to be, I always have felt that you guys want overnight success.I mean, it's what's been implied since the department of corrections and everything, that it's supposed to happen like that, and I'm not, it's not going to happen overnight for me.

NORM: Okay.

JOHN: But I don't think I'm cracked, I hope not. I have something else that I really think needs to be discussed or done. I don't like thinking about how my friend died, that really bugs me, my brother, whew.

NORM: Does it always have to be that way?

JOHN: I'm sure for a long time it will be either straight or stoned, it's hard, um . . .

NORM: And yet that's what got you going?

JOHN: There are parts that, I mean, it's still there, but it's gone. You're missing someone in life, and they're missing because they were taken, you know.

NORM: Are you up for some homework?

JOHN: Sure. (Norm hands John a quarter) Cool. You paid me. Next time I'll bring my good luck charms. Sam gives me good luck charms, but I don't have any today.

NORM: I'll give you a quarter. Here's the homework. Flip the quarter with Sandy every night; if it comes up tails, you don't smoke the next day.

JOHN: Okay.

NORM: If it comes up heads, you have a normal day. Okay?

JOHN: Okay.

NORM: Every night it's heads, tell Sandy, "I'm gonna have a normal day." Tails, no smoking until at least like Tuesday, 4 o'clock.

JOHN: Okay

NORM: Okay, and notice what's different.

JOHN: Okay.

[End of session 2]

SESSION 3

Creating a Scale

NORM: Well, let me ask you sort of an assessment question to see how we're doing here. Between 1 and 10, if 1 was where you were at when you telephoned for an appointment here—

JOHN: Okay.

NORM: Okay, that's 1, and 10 is a time when you no longer see the need for continuing therapy, where would you say you are now, between 1 and 10?

JOHN: Oh, I'd say we were almost half-way there.

NORM: Almost to about a 5?

JOHN: Yeah, 4, 4½.

NORM: Okay.

JOHN: Let's say that.

NORM: This morning, okay.

JOHN: You've given me kind of tools, you know, like the quarter thing.

NORM: Yeah?

JOHN: That's where it's, um . . .

NORM: Tell me about that.

JOHN: I've done the quarter deal. Um, I would say 75% of the time since last time. So it's been pretty consistent. I've been a little on edge because my, I totaled my truck and my Volkswagon won't be ready 'til tomorrow and I've been without a vehicle, so I've had to bum a couple of rides.

NORM: Yeah.

JOHN: So I was a little bitchy at Sandy about that.

NORM: Mmhmm . . .

JOHN: But, ah . . .

NORM: And yet with these kinds of problems, these practical everyday problems, you were still flipping the coin?

JOHN: Flipping the coin.

NORM: and . . .

JOHN: Um . . .

NORM: Following its advice?

JOHN: Yes. I went, if it read, "yes I could," I limited it, and if "no I couldn't," I went to 4 o'clock.

NORM: Okay.

JOHN: And that was pretty good because I'm building a roof system that's not just me but 3 other guys . . .

NORM: Yeah.

JOHN: That's pretty complicated.

NORM: Yeah.

JOHN: So, um, I've kept it under control.

Noticing a Solution

NORM: So, how, how did you do that?

JOHN: Um . . .

NORM: Not build the roof . . . how did you do it, not smoking pot?

JOHN: Not smoke? Um . . .

NORM: How did you do that?

JOHN: Just do it. Just can't do it today. You know, like, the doobie would come around at break, and I'd just, "Nah, I'm not, not into it today." You know, I just, no one you know is like, "Come on do it, come on."

NORM: Umhmm.

JOHN: No one minded.

NORM: So there wasn't much pressure after you said no?

JOHN: No. No, not at all.

NORM: Did that surprise you at all?

JOHN: Um, yes and no. Yes, because I figured someone would say, "What are you, wimping out today?" or, then no, because we've all kind of, we're all under the gun a little bit.

NORM: Yeah.

JOHN: The work . . .

NORM: Yeah.

JOHN: So, uh, I don't think it was a big surprise to anybody, and um, we've all been keeping them a little cool because we have evaluations that were done yesterday.

NORM: Hmmm, your company does these?

JOHN: Their foreman, so, the framing foreman does the framing crew, and the finish foreman does the finish crew, and vice versa, the painting crew . . .

NORM: And you find out about these evaluations?

JOHN: Oh, we will. I, I have to do one on myself.

NORM: Mmhmm . . .

JOHN: So, and hand it in Sunday at the company party.

NORM: Okay.

JOHN: So work's been, you know, I think I've been more on, uh, edge at home because I've been trying to, I'm trying to sell my truck, and finally the guy I thought about selling it to him in the spring decided to buy it and he was out a vehicle and edgy, and Sandy's been bitchin' and moanin' about money because I got a loan for the new car and sold my truck and she wants all the extra money.

NORM: Umhmm . . .

JOHN: Paid the bank, paid the taxes, and . . .

NORM: So, how was it you were able to say no?

JOHN: To getting high?

NORM: Yeah.

JOHN: Well, there's some sort of thing back here and here and here (points to head) just that, you know, today's not the day, you know . . .

NORM: Something just sort of clicked in?

JOHN: Right. Today you know I'm not. Last night after we went out on the ferry for dinner and everybody got tanked . . .

NORM: Um . . .

JOHN: And like today I have no intentions, I mean it felt good this morning, the food is what really kills me, when the food is bad. But, the pot smoking, it was pretty cool because no one, you know, like, if this had been a couple a years ago or high school, you know, someone would of said something and give you a little pressure, and you know, this is life, so Neil at work, he has this thing where he might have some pot, but he says, "I'm only gonna bring two joints to work," so when that's gone, you know.

NORM: Then the smoking is over?

JOHN: Right. So if he smokes one when he gets there and then smokes one on break, then by 12, you know, you just . . .

NORM: That's it?

JOHN: Yeah, you're straight by 12.

NORM: What did your wife notice that was different?

JOHN: Um, well . . . I'm not with her during the day. Well, actually on the weekend I had to make it 'til 4 o'clock. Sandy would be there, we'd flip it at night, and then, like, I would even leave it at home or I'd just put it in my lunchbox and then wait 'til 4 o'clock. But I left it home because we were all gonna meet at the overlook after work and, uh, so zoomed home real quick, I live just minutes from the job, and zoomed back, and, you know, we all like to kick back, you know, I mean, some people go and drink heavily after work, but, and, uh, I think I was more effective at work.

NORM: And, and, how could you tell that?

JOHN: There was more, maybe I was more aware of the surroundings, where I was, what I was doing. Sometimes when you're baked at work and you're just moving along, you know, you forget that something like, it's nailed but it's not completely nailed and if you're walking on the end of it you'll cantilever and . . . so a little more aware of your surroundings, you know, you're not so, so relaxed . . . And, you know, you get up there and then you start, and you're moving around, even when you're high you know, reality comes in front of you, you know, if this goes, I'm going boom, boom, boom . . .

NORM: Oh, so you were more safety conscious also?

JOHN: Yeah. Sometimes.

NORM: When you were straight?

JOHN: Yeah.

NORM: So what did your wife notice on the weekend that was different?

JOHN: Probably a little more peppy, you want to get right out and do things, and sometimes I get on these cleaning binges on the weekends when I get real bitchy and come on, all I want to do is clean house.

NORM: Yeah.

JOHN: But I was cleaning, but I didn't get bitchy,

NORM: Mmm . . .

JOHN: And I did the litter.

NORM: You did the litter?

JOHN: Whew.

NORM: You mean like kitty litter?

JOHN: Cat. Oh yeah, so . . .

NORM: So, your wife noticed that you weren't bitchy?

JOHN: Oh yeah.

NORM: Anything else she noticed?

JOHN: Um, no I don't think she said too much. I think she kind of wondered if I went and ran some errands and, you know, but I left it at home so she knew that, she looked up on the shelf and she saw it, so . . .

NORM: And anybody else that you think might have noticed even just a little difference?

JOHN: Ah, Sam probably noticed, but, you know, he doesn't know. He knows the difference but doesn't know how to explain it, but yes.

NORM: Yeah, what difference did Sam notice?

JOHN: What would he notice? I really don't know what he would notice. He probably would just kind of think, maybe he'd think something was wrong. I know, I paid him to pick up the basement, the playroom. Well, I gave him a dollar.

NORM: He did notice he got paid for picking up? And, let's see, so generally speaking, you're about a 4½?

JOHN: Yeah.

NORM: What else tells you you're about a 4½ now?

JOHN: Well, because I may not always want to flip that coin. I could just get sick of flipping the coin every night, and say, "The hell with this." There's more to learn about, more tricks. I don't want to say tricks; there's more to learn about the ways to cope and get over things than be stoned every day.

NORM: So that you know you're getting to be about half-way there because you're thinking about not using?

JOHN: Right.

NORM: Yeah, and are there other ways that you know that you're at this 4.5?

JOHN: Well, the other issue is, I don't know, I guess almost disappeared.

Creating a Progress Scale

NORM: Almost disappeared? Put that on a scale. 1 means it's as bad as it was in the past, and 10 means it is no longer a problem, it never occurs. Where are you at 1 to 10 on that one?

JOHN: Um, 6.

NORM: 6?

JOHN: Yeah. I guess one of the big reasons is that we'd uh, reevaluated our AT&T calling systems—

NORM: Oh, you have?

JOHN: So—

NORM: Okay, okay. So that's one of the things that has helped, reevaluation.

JOHN: I'm just sick of too many phone bills now.

Noticing Another Solution

NORM: Now what have you done to help that problem?

JOHN: (Pause) Nothing.

NORM: Actually, to help that solution?

JOHN: Um, nothing. I've just been, uh, I don't know. It hasn't been a thought in the past, I don't know, month or so, maybe a little longer. You know how you just get sick of things after a while, so don't do them anymore. I was sick of getting sick when I ate lobster, so I don't eat lobster anymore.

NORM: Yeah, kind of sick of feeling sick and tired.

JOHN: Because it has its advantages and maybe there isn't, uh, maybe there's no time for that anymore. I mean, I get up between 5 and 5:30, it's go to work, come home, and we've been doing a lot of things in the last month or so. It hasn't been a focal point.

NORM: Are you doing stuff with the family?

JOHN: Yeah.

NORM: Do you think that's helped to have that more a focal point of your life?

JOHN: Yeah.

NORM: Mmhmm, and yet you're at about a 6?

JOHN: Yeah, I almost could say there is recovery in sight on that.

NORM: There is?

JOHN: In sight.

NORM: In sight, so . . .

JOHN: I can see the light at the end of the tunnel.

NORM: 10 is in sight on that one?

JOHN: 10 is in sight. I think that . . .

NORM: And you'll know you're at a 10? How are you going to know?

JOHN: Um, I'll know I'm at a 10 when I think I feel comfortable about hanging out alone.

NORM: Hmm.

JOHN: You usually have two choices when you hang out alone. You can make it big and get obscene, you can sit there and watch TV, you can sit there and read, you know, oh, it's a choice, it's the only choice I want to make.

NORM: Oh, okay. Great!

JOHN: You know, I mean, I'm getting more stuff on work to read and to do, I've been cleaning more downstairs in my workshop and doing stuff there with free time, turning, instead of being nonproductive, turning it into productive.

NORM: Okay.

JOHN: You know, I think that, that situation came more from unproductive time.

NORM: Unproductive time?

JOHN: Bored, boredom time. And if I can sit, even if I can sit there and just, ever since I was little I've always loved just flipping through catalogs, you know, Penney's, Sears, L.L. Bean.

NORM: Yeah.

JOHN: Now, you know, I'm doing stuff that's productive, you know, like working down in the shop, cleaning up the house, stuff that's worthwhile.

NORM: Okay. That you also like to do, it sounds like.

JOHN: Well, also if I get stuff done and do stuff around the house, then Sandy's happy and I get liberties, you know, I get to go over to a friend's on Friday night, and . . .

NORM: So it's sort of a one hand washes the other kind of a deal?

JOHN: Yeah, yeah. And so it really hasn't been a real focal point for some time. I see the end of the tunnel, I'm not going back, I'm not pushing myself backwards, but I'm trying to push myself forwards.

NORM: Yeah. That makes sense.

JOHN: I mean, I've tried to stop smoking pot before and tried to push myself forward hard, but just never seemed to. I just kept falling backward . . .

NORM: Yeah. So it's wise to take these things quite slowly.

Searching for Goals

NORM: Sort of in the spirit of that, what do you think your next step is going to be, to go from 4½ to 5?

JOHN: Leave it at home every day.

NORM: Leave it at home every day?

JOHN: If I can work to that, and leave it at home; leave my pot at home every day, that'll be an accomplishment. Actually, that would be productive.

NORM: Yeah.

JOHN: And I think I would feel, I can see, feel and see big change.

NORM: What big change do you think you see?

JOHN: Probably more productive at work. Work will pick up and probably get even better.

NORM: So going up a notch?

JOHN: Well, there's a positive result, you know. I mean, I'll probably be more aware, I'll be more clear, and maybe it'll be hard for the guys at work to see that . . .

NORM: Mmhmm.

JOHN: Maybe it'll even be scary for them that, you know, I mean, they know I'm here, I told 'em that, you know.

NORM: Oh you have?

JOHN: So, I guess being open about it right from the beginning with them is, is I think, a plus for me because I can throw it in their face, you know, "I told you guys a while ago that this has been going on," and you know, I pulled the quarter thing on them and you know, blah, blah, blah. You know, one of them opened his Rolling Rock and then . . . swallows it down and says, "You want one?"

NORM: So, what might you notice that tells you you're at a 5?

JOHN: I'd have to become a self-manager, managing myself and being more effective with what I'm doing and not falling into a trap.

NORM: Okay.

JOHN: You know, it's not sitting down and getting baked and like, oh, just forget it, leaving the dishwater in the sink and then the dishes in there and the garbage is stinking and the litter is there and, oh, Sandy will take care of it, and taking off and not leaving a note—actually I always leave a note.

NORM: So, finishing a project is all part of this self-management that you're talking about?

JOHN: Yeah. Accomplishing the task and finding other things to do other than sitting on my dead ass and smoking.

Compliments and Homework

NORM: So, I think you're doing great!

JOHN: Really?

NORM: Yeah. I think it's fantastic!

JOHN: Well, see, I think it's justifiable by saying I'm thinking about it now, I'm more, thinking more about—

NORM: Yeah.

JOHN: —you know, what I've been doing for, you know, the last 16 years.

NORM: Mmhmm.

JOHN: I mean, now I'm Sam's soccer coach, I'm gonna have to be out there going like this, and I don't want to be going like this and (breathes in and out rapidly several times).

NORM: Yeah.

JOHN: You know, I think not only, I had someone tell me when they released me from the correctional center, a case worker there who said, "You don't need anything but to grow up and start thinking about it."

NORM: Okay, so you're doing that.

JOHN: So that's why I don't think about going out and stealing or anything like that, so, you know, that's just, that's not an option, that's not an option that I can live with.

NORM: Yeah.

JOHN: And I mean, I see if that happens, I'd just be a blowing rampage, you know, I just don't see that. I can visually see the consequences when I drive by it . . . Sam is only 6, I got to be . . .

NORM: You have a lot of years coaching soccer ahead of you.

JOHN: Yeah. And if I can go from here, down to here on my dependency, and limit it, and know how to restrict it when it's right and when it's wrong and when I'm in a safe environment, because, I mean, I don't like thinking about what would happen if I got hurt or Sam or Sandy or somebody else did . . .

NORM: Yeah.

JOHN: That's important to me.

NORM: Yeah. That's been important all along, to make those kinds of decisions.

JOHN: I think another thing, I can be driving down the street and just start crying just thinking about my brother. I think the death thing is something that I really need to get a grip on.

NORM: Umhmm.

JOHN: You know, that, that is something that is important to me.

NORM: Right.

JOHN: Because it, it, it happens every day, and it's going to be happening again in my life soon when my friend dies, and I just, I don't like thinking about people dying because that really disturbs me.

NORM: When you're at 4½ now, when . . .

JOHN: I think . . .

NORM: When are you gonna be ready to deal with the death thing?

JOHN: I don't now . . . when you get a bigger box of tissue.

NORM: A bigger box of tissue?

JOHN: Even at work, even at work it's hard to, you know, I have to, after I talk about my brother dying and telling somebody, "This is how he died," it takes me a minute to regroup. You know, you turn and you look at the guy that's over there and you see, I see my brother's face, you know, you see it there.

NORM: Yeah.

JOHN: You know, and it, I mean, that's good, I mean, I think it's good, I mean, it's not like I'm going to call Neil "Jim" or something like that. I mean, I'll never forget my brother.

NORM: But it sounds like you're getting ready to begin talking about it?

JOHN: Right. Well, I did. I started last night. We went out with Randy, who works with my wife. He's gay. I mean, I really wanted to know what my brother's life was like, so I started talking to him about it, and asked him about that type of life, and told him some of the bars that my brother used to visit in Boston when he lived there, and kind of getting a view of, he had an executive security job with this defense contractor, that was his day life, and then he had another life at night.

NORM: Yeah.

JOHN: I just wanted to make sure my brother, I guess gay people they do all that and they have anal sex and all, and I just wanted to know my brother wasn't getting hurt or anything, because, that really would, you know, even if he's not around any more I'd probably go hunting someone down.

NORM: Umhmm.

JOHN: People are people. Give them a break, they've got feelings too. I guess I'm feeling that because I think I've hurt people in the past, you know, not since, emotionally, emotionally I guess I still do it, and I need to get out of doing it.

NORM: Turn it into something good?

JOHN: Right. Like if I get mad at Sandy, I mean, I can go off the handle. I'd rather deal with the situation than carry it on and say, "You're stupid, because you're . . . " No one's stupid.

NORM: Umhmm.

JOHN: You know, I just want to be able to grip my expression, my vocal expression, sometimes with people, because sometimes it's like (smacks hands together) instead of just (smacks hands together much more gently).

NORM: Oh, I got you.

JOHN: And that in the last week or so, with this vehicle, has kind of happened a couple of times and it really, I mean, I don't punch walls, I just kind of (vocal expression of tension), you know I don't like going (same vocal expression of tension).

NORM: Right and that's why we want to take this slowly. We have to wrap up here.

JOHN: Right.

NORM: In terms of homework. I want you to continue to do what you're doing.

JOHN: Oh, I was gonna do that anyway.

NORM: Yeah. Continue to flip the coin, and let's add something to it. This time I want you to, as you flip the coin and as you follow the coin's instructions, to begin to notice when you, I guess it's a feeling, when you are feeling ready to take over, to become a self-manager, is that what you called it?

JOHN: Right.

NORM: To manage yourself.

JOHN: I'm managing myself now, but I'm not managing it, well, let's see . . . productively.

NORM: Yeah. I really want you to take this slowly. To continue as we're going now, continue the coin flip and notice those signs that you can monitor within yourself.

JOHN: Oh yeah, okay.

NORM: You've had a lot of counseling before, you've had a lot of time to think about this, and using your strengths, and like you were saying before, about you know that you've hurt other people and you're trying to turn that into something good and becoming a protector of people . . . you've had time to look at yourself.

JOHN: God, you've actually noticed that about me?

NORM: Yeah, yeah.

JOHN: Cool. That makes me feel good.

NORM: So that you can notice when you think you're gonna be ready to begin taking this project over, take it easy, take it slow.

JOHN: Right. Well, it's one nail at a time.

[End of session 3]

Two follow-up sessions were kept. The client called before the next session to cancel, saying only that he was doing okay and couldn't take the time away from work. He also called to cancel the last follow-up session, saying he was continuing to do well and did not need to reschedule. In a six-month follow-up the client reported his life was going well and he had achieved success with his goals. There were a total of five sessions.

PART II

SPECIAL TREATMENT SITUATIONS

Chapter 7

Clients Who Are "Codependent"

Many professional articles and books claim there is a personality trait or cluster of behaviors that is best described as codependent (e.g., American Society of Addiction Medicine, 1996). This is also a pervasive belief held by clinicians. However, when we closely observed these behaviors, we were startled to see that they are nothing more than attempts to insure some sense of predictability. Behaviors commonly called manipulating, controlling, and being critical were found to be an attempt to inject some sense of order to an unpredictable and often chaotic pattern of life with a problem drinker.

Everyone's daily life requires a certain amount of regularity and predictability. We often hear the spouse saying she needs to know if her husband will be coming home for dinner, for their children's school event, or for a special family occasion. Since the problem drinker's pattern is not very predictable, even to himself, she is not able to predict that the family can pile into the car at 5:30 to head for their son's little league game. In an attempt to insure and increase the certainty, the wife will remind the husband about the importance of coming home on time. Because she is not confident that he heard her, she repeats the reminding, which by now has turned into "nagging." We are all familiar with what follows the nagging. As his drinking behavior becomes increasingly erratic, she must double and triple her efforts to put some order and predictability into her life. Her attempts at a solution to the problem unfortunately just do not work. Without realizing this, she keeps trying the same problem-solving attempts without success. From her way of thinking, trying harder should work. She doubles her effort but gets no results and she becomes increasingly frustrated and angry. She soon begins to believe the problem drinker is spitefully trying to defy her. When she reaches this point of frustration, she becomes even angrier. This pattern escalates the cycle of what's not working and increases the level of anger and resentment on both sides. Pretty soon she threatens to leave him or complains loudly that she is going to "throw the bum out."

THE COIN TOSS EXPERIMENT

When we look at this behavior from a different perspective, it offers us some idea about how to be helpful to someone whose life is spinning out of control. Since we all know that only the problem drinker can do something about his drinking, all the partner can do is something about her own behavior. This is, of course, the advice given by Al-Anon, but family members often become indignant at the suggestion. They are not yet ready to accept that they are powerless to change someone else; they are not ready to see their part in the process and are still looking to the problem drinker to make their life a little easier. Spouses often vacillate between leaving the marriage and staying in the marriage, usually depending on the problem drinker's drinking habit. The pattern of blaming, admitting guilt, promising to never do it again is quite familiar. Spouses know what will follow each pattern. We have found the following homework task easily drives home the point without lecturing and preaching that only the problem drinker can change his own behavior

You can help the client whose spouse is a problem drinker reach a "teachable moment" by asking if her efforts so far have worked. Naturally, you are likely to get the answer, "No. That's why I'm here talking to you!" When she is receptive to doing something different we suggest the following experiment. Have her keep a coin next to her bed. Before going to bed each night, she is to secretly toss the coin. If it comes up heads, she is to pretend the entire next day that she has decided to stay with the problem drinker *no matter what he does.* If she gets tails, she is to pretend the entire next day that she has decided to leave the problem drinker *no matter what he does.* She is not to tell her spouse about her experiment. This task allows her the experience of detachment one day at a time. She is also to observe what she notices different about herself and about her partner and to the report on the results of the experiment at the next session.

Chapter 8

Chronic Relapsers

We all have clients we dread hearing from. Do you ever find yourself muttering, "Oh no, not him again," "Please, not her, I don't want to work with her again!" "Not that couple, they'll never learn," or "Who? I thought we discharged him from detox just last week." These and similar statements describe clients we call the chronic relapsers or, jokingly, the "frequent flyers." However, these labels lack precision in delineating this particular clinical population, and we are often left with a sense of dread and quickly think of ways to get rid of her. This is not helpful for the client or for us.

Claudia Blackborn (Blackborn, 1995) has proposed a more helpful definition of the chronic relapser. This type of client is distinguished from our other clients by the following features:

1. The client has made more than one attempt to quit drinking by participating in treatments that can be characterized by increased intensity and length. These treatment experiences have failed to make a significant difference in assisting the client to reduce or eliminate her reliance on alcohol.

2. Though the client may have experienced brief periods of abstinence, these periods were not helpful in developing a pattern that creates a useful long-term difference. Consequently, the client is not able to rely on recovery skills developed in the past to assist her with the current recovery.

3. There is a persistent pattern in which the consequences of problem drinking become increasingly negative and harmful.

4. The client's level of motivation and willingness to participate in treatment is decreased as a result of failed attempts at recovery. The client may begin to feel hopeless about herself and become increasingly reluctant to invest resources in the current attempt at recovery.

We prefer this definition. It changes our view of the client just enough to shift our helpless and hopeless feelings about these clients. Further, we find it helpful to remember:

1. It is the treatment that has failed the client, not the client who has failed treatment.

2. If nothing has worked before, the client cannot just do what works.

3. Though the client may not be noticing specific differences, life is getting harder.

4. The client has good reason to feel helpless and skeptical that any treatment experience will make a difference.

BEGIN BY GETTING A BIG HEAD START

We suggest that therapy with the chronic relapser will go better when the therapist spends less time focused on what the client must do differently and more time focused on what she *can* do differently. We also suggest that you begin doing therapy differently as early as possible this time around.

When a client calls for help, ask her if there have been previous attempts at recovery that have involved counselors, therapists, doctors, other intoxication programs, DWI programs, jails, detox hospitals, or inpatient rehabs. Be specific and ask for details. When this question is left to the general "previous treatment," clients think you are asking, "Have you ever seen anyone like me before?" The client may not understand what information you are seeking and may give you a cursory response.

When a client tells you she has had previous treatment experiences, ask what helped and what did not help. Also ask, "How long did you stay sober?" "How was that helpful?" and "What helped you stay sober?" These questions are as diagnostically useful as an ordinary search for presession (or previous) change. The answer to these questions will help you decide what you need to try and what to avoid repeating.

When your client has had previous treatment experiences and you have decided that she fits the definition of a chronic relapser, arrange for her to come to your office as soon as possible to sign information releases. In a more ordinary case the therapist would wait until the first session to have information releases signed for previous treatment records. When the therapist makes the decision that the client is a chronic relapser, additional resources must be brought into play to increase the client's chances of success. When the releases have been signed, the therapist may contact the previous treatment providers. We strongly suggest the use of e-mail, fax, or the telephone. Simply sending the release with a request for information may take weeks or months to get a reply and by then the information you obtain may be less useful.

The next step involves expanding the number of possible solutions by engaging your client's people resources. This is easily accomplished during the initial telephone call by asking, "Who else in your life is interested in your recovery?" "How can they be helpful to you?" and "What will it take to get them to come to our first session?" When speaking to someone other than the client, ask, "How would Joy say you've helped her?" followed with, "Can you come to the appointment with Joy?"

We find it helpful to include significant people in our treatment right from

• • • • • • • • • • • • • • • • • • •

Tips from the Field:

Becoming a Resource

Graduates of your program and members of Alcoholics Anonymous can be used as people resources to befriend the downtrodden alcoholic who hasn't a friend to his name.

the beginning. When we interview chronic relapsers alone, we do not get much to go on and our search for solutions can be limited by a history of what has not worked. When we involve other people we increase the possibility that a significant solution will be created.

THE FIRST SESSION

The focus of the first session is to figure out what your client is willing and able to do, determine how this will be accomplished, and enlist appropriate support from your client's people resources.

The following questions will help the therapist organize the first session in a way that maximizes the possibility of creating a workable solution. When the client has successfully stopped drinking on her own, even for a very short period, sometimes as little as half a day, focus your curiosity on the details of *how* she did that and with *what* outcome. Also discuss with the client how confident she is in repeating her solutions. Is support needed? If so, what kind? If her answers are realistic ask, "How do you know it will work this time?" or "What tells you that you can do it this time?" Let your clinical intuition and timing be the guide on which of the following questions is appropriate, and when to use which question.

1. *Who?*
   Who wants you here today?
   Who usually gets you into action, gives you a push?
   Who do you count on for support?
   Who helps you out of trouble?
   Who in your family has solved a drinking problem?
   Who, of the friends you know today, has solved a drinking problem?
   Who will be the first to notice you are different?
   Who will benefit from the changes you are making?

2. *What?*
   What do you want most?
   What do you want to be different in your life?
   What does _____ want you to do?
   What does _____ want to see changed?
   What is the minimum amount of change that is acceptable? What difference would it make?
   What will happen when you do not change?
   What will happen when you do make the changes we have talked about?
   What will be the first thing _____ will notice to say, "It's working this time"?
   What will you do when _____ notices these changes?
   What will you do when you get the urge to fall back?

***

Tips from the Field:

Quick Detox Assessment

To quickly determine when detox is needed ask, "Have you ever stopped drinking for three or four days in a row?" "What was that like?" "How did you do that?" and "Do you think you can do that now?" When your client has never stopped long enough to experience the physical effects of quitting, the CIWA-A (Clinical Institute Withdrawal Assessment-of Alcohol) scale can be a helpful decision-making tool.

What is the first small step to take?

What is it going to take to make the first step?

3. *When?*

When must these changes begin?

When will you take the first step?

When do you want people to help you?

When you begin to make these changes, what will be different?

When do you think we should meet again?

4. *Where?*

Where will you be when you first notice a difference?

Where will _____ be when (s/he) first notices a difference in you?

Where will you be next year if you do not make these changes?

Where will you be in a year when you do make these changes?

Where will you be next week after taking the first step?

5. *How?*

How will you go about making these changes?

How do you know you can do this?

How are you treated differently when you are sober?

How have you made other changes in your life?

How will you know this time is the real thing?

How will you know this is just another damn failure? Can you prevent that?

How will _____ know this is for real?

How will you keep yourself on track?

How will making a few simple changes help?

How will making these changes make life difficult for you? What do you need to do?

6. *Other*

Is there anything else you want to tell me?

Is there a question I've forgotten to ask, that you know is important?

Are there other things in your life that are important that I should know about?

You've told me how these changes will help you; are there other things you do that are helpful?

Are you willing to do some homework? How do you know you're willing? What tells you that you can do this?

As you gather information from these questions, your job is to organize the information and formulate a solution that both your client and your program can live with. Perhaps the most important contribution we can make to the treatment of the chronic relapser is to experiment with "differences." In the traditional addiction treatment, clients quickly became "patients." Addiction counselors were the experts and believed only they knew what was wrong with the patient and how to fix it. The patients were forced to comply with the experts' guidelines for treatment. When clients relapsed, they got the book thrown at them. The end result was costly, restrictive, long-term treatment that in most cases did not work. It is important to remember that clients will do what they want to do, no matter what the experts say.

We take a different approach, even with the chronic relapser. We listen to her story and help her figure out what can be different and how to do something to make the small difference happen. We also listen to our client's people resources by asking ourselves, "Who is the real customer here?" The answer might surprise you. The real customer might be a spouse who wants a partner to help out around the house, an employer who wants to help a productive employee, a probation officer who wants a law abiding citizen, or a school teacher who wants an attentive student. In each instance, when these people resources have attended the first session we have been able to help them clarify what they can do for our client and what they may have to do for themselves.

- -

Tips from the Field:

To Stop Drinking or to Start Drinking Moderately?

Abstinence may not be a realistic goal for a client who has very little hope and energy left to apply to a solution. Most clients, even those with a long history of constant relapses, may say they want to quit drinking because they know that is what the professionals want to hear. Since clients do not want to be thrown out the door, they often say what they think professionals want to hear. Sometimes we think is it kinder to help our clients by talking them out of immediately going cold turkey. It may be more realistic to aim for harm reduction rather than complete abstinence. We have often negotiated a reduced harm goal as a first step.

When clients are able to experience a little success with these smaller goals, they build up a momentum to keep going. The next steps get easier and then the client says, "Okay, now I'm ready to quit for good."

ADDITIONAL CONSIDERATIONS

1. Written contracts. When we take the time to write up a contract with our clients, we have noticed a higher rate of compliance with homework assignments. This is particularly helpful with teenagers. Be sure to spell out the contract in the client's own words, not professional jargon. The contract should also note the presence of positive behavior, not the absence of negative behavior. For instance, instead of "I will not drive after drinking," spell out, "I will make sure that someone else will drive me home when I'm drinking."

2. Teach treatment. Begin by asking, "Do you know (or, What have you been told) about the resources right here in our community?" Many clients are simply not aware of the treatment resources they have at their fingertips. No one has ever taught them what is available. Be sure your clients know all the services your facility and community offer and how to access those services. We have found it helpful to review with our clients all of the resources

that are available to them.

3. Slips and "falling off the wagon." In the recovery process, slips are inevitable. Based on their past treatment experience, many clients believe if they slip we will not want to see them again. So, we talk about what happens when our clients slip. We want them to know our position is nonjudgmental and accepting. We want to help them maintain their goal, and when they experience a setback we want to learn from them.

4. Referrals. In addition to their recovery needs, the client may need referrals to other community services or health care services. When our client believes referrals to these services would help recovery, we do what we can to make sure a good referral happens and is followed through.

5. Medication. In our view, medication can be a helpful adjunct to our treatment. Naltrexone and disulfiram (Antabuse) both work to discourage the use of alcohol. However, they work in entirely different ways. Naltrexone blocks the urge to drink and thus the subjective experience of intoxication. Disulfiram blocks the body's ability to detoxify alcohol, causing a poisoning reaction. We prefer the use of naltrexone because it carries less risk of harmful consequences. Because both drugs are prescription, a medical doctor must be consulted. Even when clients use medication, be sure to give the client credit for the progress by asking, "What are you doing to help the medication work for you?" or "What would your physician say about how you are helping your medication work for you?" or "So, what percent is the medication helping, and what percent is you helping yourself?" We want to emphasize, both directly and indirectly, that clients must take an active role in their recovery.

Chapter 9

Families as Resources

Many treatment programs consider family members as getting in the way of what the treatment program is trying to accomplish with the problem drinker. We believe this is based on the concept of individual responsibility and that only the person with the problem can do something about finding and implementing a solution. Many research findings indicate that a supportive family and social environment is crucial not only for initial recovery but also for maintaining the recovery process. In addition, we have found it useful to involve family members when the aftereffects of the problem drinking are felt more keenly by the family members than by the problem drinker. This stands to reason, since the problem drinker is in the fog more often than the nonabusing family members. Our motto, which we have learned from many wise client-teachers, is, "Alcoholism is his problem but the solution belongs to all of us."

We define families to include not only parents and children, but also spouses, friends, neighbors, and relatives—anyone our clients describe as their family. Our definition of family is not limited to biological or legal connections, but includes the networks of people who comprise an emotional support system.

FAMILIES AS RESOURCES FOR RECOVERY

Family members have a tremendous amount of information about the problem drinker that can be helpful when tapped in a solution-building manner. Remember that while some families suffer silently, out of shame, some are not so silent, out of frustration with the problem drinker's wasted potential and unfulfilled dreams. When discussing a family member who needs to be in recovery, most families tell us about the enormous potential being wasted. Family members have a huge reservoir of care, love, and loyalty. Our task is to utilize these resources to the most common good. To do this we must be able to get family members involved!

1. Ask your client who has been most helpful in her attempts to manage the problem.

2. Ask your client how we can get this person to help her again.

3. Follow your client's cue and allow her to invite this person to come to sessions, either jointly or individually.

4. When a family member comes to a session,
   - Indicate how helpful he has been in the client's view.
   - Ask what he knows about the client that has kept him hanging in there and not giving up on her like others have.
   - Discover what the client is like when she is sober. Be persistent with details of the client's behavior and her interactions with this family member.
   - Find out what he notices about the client's successful strategies to stay sober.
   - Ask what it will take to get the client to maintain the successful strategies. Discuss her social, occupational, and family environments and how they support and encourage her sobriety.
   - Ask your client what she needs to do to keep these supportive people in her life.

5. Make sure you maintain contact with this supportive family network and learn what the client is doing right that she has such supportive people in her life even after all the years of drinking.

FAMILY MEMBERS NEED TO DO SOMETHING DIFFERENT

Whenever we listen to a family we are amazed at the sameness of the attempted solutions that didn't work. The words may vary but the behavior patterns seem the same. After giving much credit for their attempts to solve the problem and recognizing their frustration, anger, and resentment at the problem drinker, we gently and persistently ask, "What do you suppose Doreen would say that you have all done to try to be helpful to her?" Answers to this question are usually spoken in similar words: lecturing, preaching, nagging, begging, pleading, pointing out mistakes, pointing out the harm drinking is causing, threatening, bargaining, the silent treatment, sarcasm, and so on. Since the reason the family is sitting across from you is related to these failed attempts at helping Doreen do what is good for her, and Doreen, however, has not been persuaded to stop drinking, you can ask, "How well have these things worked?" Families usually answer with frustration, "They haven't worked, that's why we came to talk to you!" or, since these logical attempts have not worked, they decide that Doreen must be beyond hope. We have found that when families see that what they are doing is not working, they are able to stop doing it. Often stopping the attempted solution that did not solve the problem is enough to produce a new pattern of behavior, even though it may not immediately solve the problem of the problem drinker. When families stop what isn't working, the possibility for new relationship patterns to emerge is created.

• •

Tips from the Field:

SFT Central Philosophy

If it isn't broke don't fix it. Once you know what works, do more of it. If it doesn't work don't do more of it—do something different.

Tips from the Field:

Competency-Based Family History

Traditionally, in the medical community an individual or family history was taken to discover everything that was wrong to give the expert doctors information that could lead to a diagnosis and treatment plan. When the substance abuse field adopted the medical approach, it went overboard in its attempts to discover every family skeleton in the closet. When the therapist does not balance the successes and failures of a family, it has the effect of highlighting only the pathologies, deficiencies, family alcoholics, suicides, child molesters, abusers, and failed marriages. This is enough to depress anyone and tends to give the storyteller a feeling of hopelessness.

We contend that our clients do not need to be discouraged; instead, they need to feel hopeful. Such hope and optimism can be generated by having our clients talk about the side of the family that has successfully overcome problems and tell us about how these family members pulled their lives together.

Ask about how Uncle Joe stopped drinking, how Grandpa held a marriage together for 50 years in spite of Grandma's drinking, about how Cousin Ken decided to go cold turkey one day and how he hasn't touched a drop in 10 years, and how Cousin Bea has quietly learned to limit her drinks to no more than two per day. Our history taking includes what these people in our client's family tell her and what kind of family traits she might have inherited that will help her overcome her problem drinking and how she recognizes these traits in action in her daily life.

WHEN AND HOW TO INCLUDE FAMILY MEMBERS

If you discover early in treatment, perhaps in the first session, that a family member was the motivating force for getting the client into treatment, immediately recruit that person as a resource. As the treatment progresses in a positive direction and you discover another family member has had an important role in initiating and maintaining changes, immediately recruit that family member as a resource. These family members need not be the authority figures in the client's life. A child's begging may be more influential than the spouse's nagging. Children can be recruited as resources without fear of parentifying them. They are already trying to help; we can help them learn new skills so they can be really helpful and continue to be children.

FAMILIES ARE DYNAMIC, NOT STATIC

It is commonly believed that family members are afraid of the positive changes the client is making and are prone to "sabotage" the effort at recov-

• • • • • • • • • • • • • • • • • • • •

Tips from the Field

One of our colleagues says, "Blood is thicker than therapy." We agree!

Hearing the Story "from the Horse's Mouth"

If a family is returning to your program but is new to you, resist the temptation to read the record before seeing them for the first time. The record of their previous treatment is the therapist's version of what she and the family cocreated in therapy. The family may have a different story to tell. When a therapist reads the record of a previous treatment before seeing the family, she may become biased toward the previous therapist's description. Be prepared to see the family differently, or at least accept the family's description of their lives, either good or bad. You may open the session by asking, "So what's different in your family since you came to see us last year?"

ery. This is not a very helpful way of conceptualizing our client's family. This thinking can lead the therapist to be guarded against family members or suspicious of their intentions, and consequently to try to protect the client from harm they may inflict. Practically speaking, it would be impossible to protect our client since he will be back with his family before long, and they must be able to interact with each other in a supportive manner.

Since we see the family as a valuable resource to our client, we have a more positive and useful way of viewing the family: The family is a fluid, organic, and dynamic organization that changes over time simply because human beings constantly change. The implication of this view for treatment is that the family you met six months ago may be very different now, even though they may outwardly appear to be the same. Prepare yourself to notice that something is slightly different than before. When a therapist is open to this view she can begin to look for ways the family is changing. Albert Einstein said, "We see what we believe." We encourage you to look for small details of what is different in the way they interact with each other. Often families do not notice these details of change themselves and you need to point them out, particularly when the change is for the better. Follow up on these observations with questions about how they have made these changes, how these changes have helped, and what they have learned about themselves from making these changes.

When we observe positive changes in the family as a unit or in individuals in the family, we make a point of asking, "I notice that you all seem more relaxed and seem to look healthier; I am wondering what has been going well since you were here before?" "How do you explain that your family is getting along better?" and "What do you suppose your best friend would say is going better in your life?"

When we notice the family or the client is doing worse, it is also obvious to them that things are going downhill. One helpful way to handle such a problem is by asking, "I remember you as perky and feisty with lots of sparks; I wonder what happened to that part of you?" and "What do you suppose _____ would say would be good for you to do now with your life?" If they persist in talking about how terrible life has been since the last session, ask, "How have you coped?" and "How come it's not much worse?" In addition you might consider asking about what part of their life is worse and what part is a little less bad, what part of the week (or month) is bad and what part is better.

CREDIT FAMILY MEMBERS FOR ANY POSITIVE SUCCESS

Many therapists detest working with families, preferring to work with only the problem drinker. Many cognitive behavioral models even imply that working with family members is a nuisance and interferes with treatment protocols (Hester & Miller, 1989). Obviously, we believe differently. We believe that the success of the treatment must be proved in the real world of the client's life, not in the therapy room. As one homeless substance abuser explained the numerous failures of 30-day inpatient treatments, "It's gotta work on the streets, not inside the hospital walls."

We have also found that in certain cases it is imperative that we work with families or all the hard work of recovery will have little importance. Many programs unwittingly alienate and blame family members for the problem drinker's inability to maintain sobriety. Frequently, the problem drinker also blames the family for his inability to stay sober. There are many instances in which the inpatient treatment seemed very effective, but as soon as the client returned home he began drinking again. Unless family members are more supportive, the recovery is an uphill battle. To address this problem we always link any credit for the successful recovery of our clients to what the family members are doing that is helpful. We do this by assuming that all the family members have positive intentions until proven otherwise. Regardless of how negative, blaming, or otherwise unproductive a family member's behavior is, we give him the benefit of the doubt and are generous with our positive regard for him. We remember that all family members are doing what they believe is helpful for our client. Believing this makes it easier to get on their side to encourage them to be helpful in ways they might not have thought about before or to show them that they may need to do something different. We believe that the most important gift we can offer our client and her family is hope. In order to offer this important gift, we must first have hope for them.

LOOK FOR WAYS TO REDUCE THE INTENSITY AND FREQUENCY OF ANGER

When Barbara was admitted to treatment the first time, her husband and children breathed a sigh of relief. The admission had been a long time in coming. Many harsh and angry words had been spoken as Barbara disappointed her family with broken promises and outrageous drunken behavior. When she relapsed after five years of recovery, her husband went ballistic and her children refused to talk to her. Many nights, with slurred words Barbara would plead for her family's love and understanding. In disgust, frustration, and anger they would each, in their own way, demand that the only way she could be loved would be to first get sober. Even after she admitted herself to treatment for the second time, Barbara's family kept their distance. They were mad at her and wanted her to feel it.

The client's family will be part of her life long after the treatment is over. Your client will need continued support, encouragement, and cooperation from her family throughout her lifetime. The following are useful guides to reduce the intensity and frequency of family member's anger toward the problem drinker.

1. View the family member's anger as valid, reasonable, and normal given the circumstances and the history of suffering brought on by the problem drinking.

2. Reframe the anger as a result of disappointment, pain, and frustration at seeing much potential go to waste. Anger is a sign of deep caring and faith in the problem drinker's ability to do better.

3. Anger is the other side of love. If the family members did not care about the problem drinker, they would not bother to become angry. View the anger as passion and help the family members find more helpful ways to express it.

4. Ask the family members if the angry outbursts have produced the kind of results they wanted. If the answer is yes, find out how it was helpful for both the family and the problem drinker. If you agree with the positive results, find out if the problem drinker wants the expression of anger to continue, and in what manner it needs to continue to be helpful. If the answer is no, suggest that it is time for the family members to do something different. When this approach does not work, ask to see each family member separately. This allows space and energy to explore ways to do something differently in order to produce the desired outcome.

5. When anger persists in the family and the family has decided the anger isn't really getting them what they want, ask what each is hoping to accomplish by expressing his or her anger. A frequent answer is: "I want him to learn how much he put me through!" Follow up with another question, "Suppose he does; what do you want him to do differently?" The usual answer is, "I want him to apologize!" Continue by asking, "All right, suppose he does; how would it be helpful?" and "What difference would it make for you?" Conclude by asking, "What's the last thing (the problem drinker) would expect you to do (to be helpful)?" Focus on what the family member is really seeking. Repeated venting of anger is not only unproductive, it is also counterproductive. It makes the target the of anger, the problem drinker, defensive, and usually he either withdraws or becomes offensive with a counterattack, thus escalating the cycle of anger and mutual blaming.

6. See the anger as a means to something else the family really wants. Focus on the positive things that the family is doing and encourage positive interactions, which occur when there is less anger. Help the family do more of what is already working, even just a little.

COUPLES IN RECOVERY CHECKLIST

Our couples in recovery checklist is a good tool for helping clients quickly move away from the blaming (see appendix). This checklist is similar to the recovery checklist for individuals. It encourages couples to cooperatively assess issues that show healthy traits of a couple's life together. Once each item has been assessed, the form asks them to cooperatively indicate three of the items where a little improvement would make a big difference. Even though couples ordinarily identify items that are trouble spots in the relationship, they do so in a way that gives them a sense of hope that the problems can be solved. We also do not miss the opportunity to point out successful problem-solving skills used in completing this exercise. This can also become a guide for the session about how they usually solve problems, what works and what does not work, and the next step they might take to build upon existing solution skills.

WHAT TO DO WHEN YOU DISCOVER CHILD ABUSE

First of all, the reporting of child abuse results in relatively few substantiated cases, as legally defined by the child protection agency. In reality, more parents or caretakers are found to be neglectful than abusive of the children, and up to 80 percent of substantiated cases are neglect rather than outright abuse (Children's Protective Service, 1996; Bruner, 1995). This gives us some perspective on the issue of the legal mandate of reporting that almost all states require in the United States. We must also be mindful that the allegation of child abuse is quite different from the substantiation of child abuse, which is somewhere between 20 and 30 percent of all investigated cases.

Even in alleged sexual abuse cases it is very difficult to substantiate (in legal terms) child sexual abuse. Only a small portion, estimated to be 3–6 percent of all substantiated cases, of those accused of child sexual abuse are actually prosecuted and serve prison terms (Bruner, 1995). We want to remind you of this reality in order to underline the difficulty of establishing the legal recourse. The majority of the cases need to be handled as issues in treatment rather than as issues for the courts.

• •

Questions from the Field:

"What do you do when you suspect sexual abuse?"

We believe it is not a good idea to entertain the suspicion of child abuse, even sexual abuse, unless you have some concrete, documentable evidence that tells you that you are right. A therapist's hunch can misfire and damage the therapeutic relationship when used inappropriately. The abuse of children, sexual abuse in particular, is difficult to document in most situations. Documentation means that if the allegation is challenged in a court of law, it must be able to withstand such scrutiny.

Rather than becoming suspicious, we suggest you state your confusion. For example, when your client tells you something that gives you the strong indication that his child is being abused in some way, and yet when you pursue it, he denies it, you can say, "I am really confused about what you are saying. Perhaps you can clear up some of my confusion. Most people would interpret your touching your stepdaughter as inappropriate. The way you described it just now can be called sexual abuse. What do you think?" This kind of tentative language invites the client to clarify things for you and for himself as well. If your suspicions continue, you can either tell your client you must file a report with the proper authorities, or privately contact the proper authority anonymously, and without using the client's name describe the situation to learn what steps you can take to help clarify the matter.

We agree with our colleague Brian Cade (personal communication, 1995), who says, "Mandatory reporting is not a therapeutic act but it can be done therapeutically." In fact, we would go one step further and contend that mandatory reporting need not interfere with your treatment considerations. We suggest the following steps:

1. When the issue of sexual or physical abuse is brought to your attention, calmly state to the client that you are obligated to report to the proper authority. State this in a matter-of-fact tone of voice and manner. Do not act shocked or panicked about the report of abuse. Continue to discuss the topic by asking what steps have already been taken since the discovery of the abuse, which steps have been helpful, and what the client expects the outcome to be from the steps that have been taken.

2. Immediately ask, "Do you want to call the protective service or should we do it together?" The tone of your voice and your mannerisms should not betray any ambivalence about this topic. The reporting of abuse should be handled as if you were making a referral for a medical checkup.

3. Discuss not only what to report, but also how and when the report will be done. Who will do what part of the report and the follow-up steps after the report is made should also be made clear. Make sure the report indicates that the client is currently in treatment. Take steps to insure the safety of the child.

4. After the report is made, do not forget to do the planned follow-up. Your follow-up will send a message to the client that you are not going to abandon her. You believe that reporting the child abuse is part of a solution, and you are optimistic that there is a way to get back to a better level of functioning from a problem this serious. Again, maintain your trust that life will get better.

5. Always maintain a helpful posture with the client and do not lose sight of what your client wants from her life and from you.

WHEN PARENTS ARE PROBLEM DRINKERS, KIDS CAN STILL HAVE A HEALTHY CHILDHOOD

The popular theory about children raised in the home of a problem drinker is grim and pessimistic. According to this view children are raised into rigid roles that do not allow them the flexibility to effectively meet their needs. This theory encourages therapists to label the children as either a "hero," "scapegoat," "lost child," or "mascot." These family roles are thought to be maladaptive for coping with life in a family with alcohol problems. Children in these roles are considered to be at great risk to become the next generation of problem drinkers. We do not find this view helpful because it prejudices the therapist to see only what's wrong in a family. It also does not coincide with our clinical experience.

While working with 15-year-old Tom, a problem drinker following in his father's footsteps, who could have easily been labeled a family scapegoat, we discovered he had developed a tender and supportive relationship with his younger brother. He explained that he wanted to help his kid brother avoid the mistakes he had made. Though this young man was causing his mother many problems, he was able to make a positive contribution to his brother's childhood.

Likewise, Fred, whose father committed suicide before he was born and, as he puts it, "My mother gave me four stepfathers. Two physically abused me; one hit me so hard when he was drunk that I can't hear out of my left ear." Another of the stepfathers sexually abused his sister. At 17, Fred had the common sense to leave home and join the army. Eventually Fred earned a doctorate degree and maintains a loving relationship with his children and grandchildren. Fred turned out to be a gentle, loving, and thoughtful man. Above all, when he drinks, he drinks moderately.

Tom, Fred, and hundreds like them are our expert mentors, who teach us how to help children have a healthy childhood. They have taught us that all is not lost when a child grows up with a parent who is a problem drinker. These children have shown us which behaviors are helpful to them, the most common being a parent giving his time, attention, direction, and protection. We encourage adult clients who have children to focus on the positive contributions they can make in the lives of their children. When clients set aside time for special play with their children they often report it helps their recovery. A child calls for her parent's attention with, "Watch this, Daddy!" and it only takes a moment to look up and acknowledge the child's accomplishment. Jim, a parent, new to recovery, quickly became adept at directing his child to, "Do your homework" and "Try choking up on your bat, it will make your swing quicker." When parents recover, children relax their guard and expect protective commands like, "Don't talk to strangers" and "Look both ways before crossing the street."

Our client's children have also taught us that they are very resourceful. When they are not in an ideal situation they get support from many other places. We encourage the therapist working with a family to be aware of family members, kind and caring teachers, neighbors, and family friends who spontaneously provide care to the children with no fanfare or flag waving.

When clients report having serious problems caring for their children, therapists can help by taking a family history based upon the family's success stories. For example, in a recent interview with a problem drinker we were pleased to discover both a brother and a sister who were successfully overcoming drinking problems and were more than happy to help with the children.

CASE EXAMPLE: WE WERE TEMPTED TO THINK THE SITUATION WAS HOPELESS!

Juanita admitted to being drunk most of her days and spending them in bed, passed out, only going out of the house to attend to her numerous medical problems. She was forced to seek help by her physician, who threatened to refuse medical care if she didn't take care of her drinking problem. When asked about her family, she reported that all four children got As and Bs and never missed a day of school. Amazed by this, we wondered out loud how they were able to achieve such success. Juanita agreed with us that even she was amazed at how well they were doing and was very proud of their achievements. We learned that the children's father, Marcus, was a drug dealer who did not use the stuff he sold. He was the "responsible" parent who made sure that the children did their homework. Marcus attended each child's parent-teacher conferences and all of the school's special events. This did not fit our stereotyped view of alcohol-abusing or drug-dealing parents.

We were amazed that Juanita showed up sober for her first 10:00 A.M. appointment. She explained that whenever she has a doctor's appointment, she makes sure that she is sober until after the appointment. Aha! The second appointment was made for 11:00 A.M.; the third, for 12:00; then 1:00 P.M., and so on. Sure enough, Juanita kept sober until after the appointment every single time. She began to talk about wanting to be independent and to make her own decisions about spending the money she received from SSI. She eventually went shopping to select her own dress, learned to stand up against her mother and the domineering, abusing Marcus, who were always telling her what to do. She eventually left Marcus.

We continue to be amazed that in the midst of all this, her four children kept going to school and earning good grades, and showed no sign of "dysfunction" while navigating through times that were difficult for everyone.

CASE EXAMPLE: A DEMONSTRATION OF SOLUTION-FOCUSED THERAPY WITH A COUPLE

Insoo conducted this clinical consultation during a workshop as a demonstration of the use of solution-focused therapy with a couple in early recovery. Betty and Dave have four young children between the ages of 2 and 8. Dave has only recently returned home after Betty insisted he move out and stop drinking. The other therapists that make up Dave and Betty's treatment team are in the audience, helping Insoo by participating as a reflecting team.

Creating a Scale

INSOO: Let's say on a scale of 1 to 10, 10 means that you feel like meetings with Jim have been very helpful for you and you feel like you can go on with your life on your own without having to meet with Jim. That stands for 10. 1 stands for how bad things were when you first decided to start meeting with Jim. Where would you say things are at, between 1 and 10, right now?

BETTY: 3

INSOO: (To Dave) How about you? What would you say?

DAVE: 6

INSOO: Okay.

DAVE: Compared to where I was.

INSOO: Right. That's what I'm talking about. (To Betty) Are you talking about family life in general or are you talking about yourself? The 3, is that 3 for everybody or for yourself?

BETTY: I don't know, I think maybe for myself.

INSOO: For yourself. (To Dave) And I suspect you were talking about yourself as well?

DAVE: Correct.

INSOO: If I were to ask you to put a number on family life as a whole, on a 1-to-10 scale, where would you say things are right now?

DAVE: About a 6.

INSOO: (To Betty) How about for you?

BETTY: I'd say about a 5.

INSOO: So, as a family, as a whole you're pretty much in agreement. (To Dave) It sounds like you are more than half-way there . . . for you.

DAVE: Right.

INSOO: (To Betty) And you feel like you're about half-way there?

BETTY: Yes.

DAVE: I was pretty low down. I was drinking vodka and other things. I really slowed down. I'd been at a complete stop for a while there. I had a few setbacks.

INSOO: How long did you stop completely?

DAVE: About nine weeks.

Insoo decides to focus on "complete stop" instead of on "a few setbacks." Notice how each setback is separated from the other. We believe this detail highlights the client's sense of control over his alcohol use as well as addresses his investment in his marital and family relationship.

INSOO: Wow.

DAVE: Yes. And the last couple of weeks I've had a couple of small setbacks. Nothing like I used to.

INSOO: Really? You mean your setbacks are different than they used to be?

DAVE: Correct.

INSOO: Wow.

DAVE: I've been separated from my family about four months now. We just got back together.

INSOO: You just got back together? When?

DAVE: About two weeks ago.

INSOO: (To Betty) Is that right?

BETTY: Yes.

INSOO: So you must have seen signs that Dave was doing better?

BETTY: I did. He was in jail for 30 days and of course he couldn't have setbacks. And of course things were really good. He was sober. He was clean. He promised me that that was it, no more, and as soon as he moves in we have a couple of setbacks.

INSOO: So it's been about a couple of weeks, you said?

BETTY: Yes.

INSOO: And in that time you had a couple of setbacks?

BETTY: Yes.

INSOO: Would you agree with Dave that these are small setbacks compared to what he used to have before that?

BETTY: They're small setbacks, but I feel that they lead to bigger things.

INSOO: Sure. You're worried that this might lead to a big setback.

BETTY: Right. One turns into two and two turns into four.

INSOO: (To Dave) You seem to be pretty convinced this was a small setback.

DAVE: Compared to what I used to be.

Discovering Solutions

INSOO: How is it that you are able to have small setbacks instead of big setbacks?

DAVE: I was working on trying to stay with my family, get back together with them. It was pretty hard being without them for that period of time.

INSOO: How long were you separated?

BETTY: Four months.

INSOO: Right. Four months. So the four months was hard for you?

DAVE: Very hard. Things just got worse instead of better when I was separated from them.

INSOO: So you do better when you're with your family?

DAVE: Not in the past but hopefully now in the future. Before I used to take off for a few days. The family life wasn't that great then, but I'm trying to improve on it.

INSOO: I want to get back to this. Betty, how do you explain that you are up to 3?

BETTY: As far as family life?

INSOO: As far as you go. The family was about a 5.

BETTY: I guess because I have a lot of doubts, a lot of insecurities.

INSOO: About?

BETTY: About life in general. Life without alcoholism, drugs.

INSOO: And in spite of that you moved up to 3. How did that happen?

BETTY: Because I saw a little bit of improvement.

INSOO: In Dave?

BETTY: Right.

Relational Questions

INSOO: Is that right? She saw some improvement in you?

DAVE: I think so. I could communicate a little better. Before I was shut off and didn't want to talk. I like to talk to her a little bit more now.

INSOO: Is that right? You communicate a little bit better?

BETTY: (Pause) Yes. (Laughs)

INSOO: Yes? You have a way to go?

BETTY: A long way to go.

INSOO: Right. (To Dave) What did Betty do that was helpful so that you were able to communicate with her even a little better? What did she do to be helpful to you?

Phrasing questions this way assures that Betty has done something to help improve the communications. It is obvious that Betty believes that Dave has a long way to go. However, since Betty agreed that "a little bit" is better, giving credit to Betty will help keep her motivated to continue working. Notice how Dave credits Betty for having forced him to leave the family home. It is important for the therapist to support and validate each partner's view of how each experiences his or her lifes both together and separately!

DAVE: By leaving me it made me want to communicate more because I wanted to work things out.

INSOO: So leaving was helpful?

DAVE: Yes. It hurt me a lot and I wanted to express my feelings to her.

INSOO: (To Betty) Is that right?

BETTY: I think so. To me it's like a cycle. It's like I left so he wanted to communicate more. He wanted to work things out. He was in jail during that time and everything else. Once he's back in our family again it seems like the communication has gone down. Sometimes I think we get along better when he is out of the house.

INSOO: So I guess you have reason to be cautious about the future?

BETTY: Yes.

INSOO: Because you have had many of these?

BETTY: Right.

INSOO: So what do you need to see from Dave for you to say, "Maybe this time is different?"

BETTY: What I need personally is I need Dave to completely give up alcohol.

INSOO: Altogether.

BETTY: Altogether. Not one sip, not one beer, nothing. That's not acceptable to me anymore because I've seen in the past 8½ years that it doesn't ever stop with one. And communicating more!

INSOO: So no more alcohol, communicating with you more. What else?

BETTY: Be attentive to my feelings and needs. When I say, "I want to talk," it's "Well, we'll talk tomorrow." Then tomorrow I'll say, "Can we talk?" and it's "Let's just drop it." When something is bothering me I need him to listen to me and be attentive to me.

INSOO: So that's gotten a little bit better? Up to a 3?

BETTY: A little bit.

INSOO: Just a little bit. About 3. So what will push it up to 4? Maybe 3.5?

BETTY: How I feel today, at this point, I have no trust. I have no trust. I hate to say that, it hurts me to say that, but I think the only way I can trust him and move it up to possibly a 4 is for him to be on medication for alcoholism.

INSOO: You mean something like Antabuse?

BETTY: Yes.

INSOO: That will increase your trust in him?

BETTY: Yes.

INSOO: So that will move you up to 3.5 or 4?

BETTY: Maybe about a 5.

INSOO: About a 5. Okay. (To Dave) What do you think about that?

DAVE: I agree with that.

INSOO: You agree with that?

DAVE: Yes. I've been drinking for about 20 years now. The people I hang around with and work with, they all drink, so it's hard to stay away from it. A lot of peer pressure it seems like. All my peer pressure should come from my family.

BETTY: He should hang around his family instead of his friends.

INSOO: You agree with her it sounds like?

DAVE: That's something we've talked about in just the last couple of days. I've just got to stay with my family and things will be a lot better.

INSOO: So what do you have to do so that happens?

DAVE: Give up my friends.

INSOO: Oh. That's not going to be easy.

DAVE: If I lose them again (his family) it will be pretty tough.

INSOO: But how are you going to do that? Giving up all your friends is not going to be easy.

DAVE: No. Just try staying home. My family will be my friends.

Asking, "Suppose . . . "

INSOO: Suppose if this past couple of weeks since you've gotten back together, if that were to maintain, what would that be like? Let's say if it were maintained for 10 months or so?

BETTY: The way the past two weeks have been?

INSOO: Yes.

BETTY: I don't like the way the past two weeks have been.

INSOO: You don't?

BETTY: No.

INSOO: So what about the past two weeks was good and what was not good?

BETTY: He made empty promises to me. Empty promises like, "I'm not drinking anymore. I'm not going to hang around those people anymore. We're going to do things as a family." It's like he's had two or three setbacks since he moved in, which totally blew my hope. And just the attitude he has toward me. I feel like he doesn't like being there with us. I feel he's angry. We get into verbal fights in front of the kids. That's uncalled for. That's the reason I left four months ago: a lot of fighting. Him not coming home for days at a time. Of course, while he was doing that I was angry with the kids. I was taking it out on the kids because there was no one else there to take it out on. I feel us going back into that same cycle again, and I'm not putting my kids through that for another . . . I was in it for almost nine years. I'm not doing it for another nine.

INSOO: Of course. (To Dave) So it sounds like you have a tough job?

DAVE: Yes.

INSOO: To convince Betty that it's different this time.

DAVE: It's just been real stressful the last couple of weeks with four real young children.

BETTY: But we're still going to have four children in three months. Whether it's been stressful because we've had four children this past two weeks . . . we're still going to have them.

DAVE: (Laughs) I don't know. It's just something I'll have to work on.

INSOO: Do you have some plans about how you're going to do this?

DAVE: Yes.

INSOO: You do?

DAVE: I'm going to get put on Antabuse.

INSOO: You want to go on Antabuse?

DAVE: Yes.

INSOO: So, you agree with Betty on that. So that's the first step you want to take. What else?

DAVE: Just by staying home with the family and doing more with them.

INSOO: You sound confident about that.

DAVE: I do.

INSOO: You do. That you can do this. Stay home and sort of get rid of your old friends.

DAVE: Right. I have said that in the past too, but I'm a little bit more confident this time than last time.

INSOO: Really? What's changed this time?

DAVE: I saw what it's like being by myself now. It's a lot more enjoyable being with my family than it was out drinking with my friends. It's a lot lonelier by myself.

INSOO: (To Betty) What do you think about what he said?

BETTY: Right now I'm kind of at, "I'll believe it when I see it." I mean, he'd be gone for four days and he'd walk in the door, "Hi! I'll never do this again. I promise." Then a week later he goes, "I'll never do this again, I promise." It's my fault because I let it go on for so long. I kept saying, "Okay, next time this is it," and then it would happen again and I'd be like, "Okay, next time this is it."

INSOO: So what's different about it this time?

BETTY: I don't think there's anything different about it this time.

INSOO: About Dave.

BETTY: Yes. He says he's going to stay in with the family and la dee da dee da. He said all this before and never did anything about it. If he gets on the Antabuse and stays with it and goes to AA meetings then I'd feel good about it.

INSOO: So you want him to what? Go on Antabuse, go to AA meetings, and that will make you feel better?

BETTY: Yes.

INSOO: Has he done this before? Gone on Antabuse?

BETTY: There was always some reason why he couldn't do it. He went to AA meetings a couple of times. I don't know if he had to go.

DAVE: It is part of my therapy program. I haven't gone to AA meetings for about a week. They do help me quite a bit. I've never gone in the past with this.

INSOO: You say that going to AA was helpful.

DAVE: Very helpful.

INSOO: What about it?

Rather than automatically accepting the fact that going to AA is helpful, Insoo wants to know what it is about going to AA that is helpful to Dave. This line of questioning forces the client to describe his personal meaning of going to AA and frequently opens up additional possibilities for achieving the same meaning. Also notice how Insoo builds consensus and agreement between the couple as the session moves on, thus creating a joint view out of what had been colliding and opposite views.

DAVE: Just talking to people of all walks of life that are just like me. They weren't just a lot of drunks sitting in the corner. There were professional people of all different ages lending a lot of support. People that have stopped for years. I had no desires to drink at all then and, like I said, I was in a work release program and I didn't drink, of course. Then I started to hang out with my friends again and I drank a couple of times since then. Nothing real bad or nothing major, to myself. To her, one drink is bad enough. But it's not compared to what it used to be. I need to get back into going to AA. I'd like to go every night but she works at night sometimes.

INSOO: So that means you have to watch the kids?

DAVE: Correct.

Search for Exceptions

As the following dialogue indicates, searching for what was different about the setback this time reveals a considerable degree of control.

INSOO: I'm curious about a couple of things. You said this time your setback was smaller than in the past. How did you manage to have a smaller setback this time than other times?

BETTY: Because it was for one night instead of two or three.

INSOO: How come it was only one night?

DAVE: I just don't want to get back into that cycle. I went out and had a few beers with some friends. It wasn't anything. I didn't get involved with other drugs. It was usually doing drugs like cocaine that would keep me gone for three days.

INSOO: So this time you didn't do any drugs, just alcohol?

DAVE: Correct.

INSOO: And that's a change for you?

DAVE: Correct.

INSOO: Wow. So you decided this time you're not going to do any drugs.

DAVE: I've never intended to do that.

INSOO: Is that right?

DAVE: That's right. That's really cost me a lot financially and emotionally and the family stability.

INSOO: (To Betty) Are you convinced about that? That Dave does not want to do any cocaine?

BETTY: No.

INSOO: You're not convinced about that. Did you know about this? That he did not want to do drugs this time?

BETTY: I've heard that.

INSOO: You've heard that before?

BETTY: I mean, I'd like to support him and have confidence in him. I want to. But like I said, I don't have any trust. I don't have any trust. But I know if he's on Antabuse and he's not drinking, then I know he's not going to do cocaine.

INSOO: (To Dave) There are a couple of other things I'm curious about. How come you didn't do drugs or alcohol for 30 days while you were in jail?

DAVE: There was a big incentive there because they do random tests. Also, just not with my friends. I was a lot lonely in jail and on the work release program, knowing I wanted to get out and be with them. That's something I had to do.

INSOO: So you were able to stick with that.

DAVE: Correct. After drinking for 20 years, I was hoping there wouldn't be any setbacks and I thought there would be. It's not easy. Especially with the people I hang out with.

INSOO: So you seem to think that it's the people you hang out with.

DAVE: I'm one of them too, so.

INSOO: (To Betty) Would you agree with that? It's the people he hangs out with that's more difficult for him than himself?

BETTY: Dave falls into a lot of peer pressure. He's a follower. I don't know if he's afraid to say, "No, I don't do that anymore."

Constructing a Solution

INSOO: Somehow you managed only one day of drinking?

DAVE: Right.

INSOO: So you must have said no to somebody?

DAVE: Right.

INSOO: How?

DAVE: Because of the cocaine. That always turns into three days.

INSOO: So you know that about yourself.

DAVE: Right.

INSOO: So how were you able to say no to cocaine? I'm sure the pressure was there, too.

DAVE: Yes. I'm just stronger about not doing that right now. I've seen my best enemy.

INSOO: You're more certain about the cocaine?

DAVE: Correct. If there is a drug that would make me stop doing that, I would do that too.

INSOO: So you think that going on Antabuse will also help you say no to cocaine?

DAVE: That's the only time I ever do that is if I drink. Once I start drinking, I have a few beers and it leads to it.

INSOO: So the alcohol is the road to cocaine?

DAVE: For me. I think a little bit straighter than if I'm drinking and stuff, of course.

INSOO: So this is how you're thinking about things. So you sorted things out for yourself.

DAVE: Correct.

INSOO: (To Betty) Did you know about this?

BETTY: Yes.

INSOO: You know about that? That it's the alcohol that makes him say yes to cocaine. I see. So you agree with Dave that once he says no to alcohol he's less likely to—

BETTY: Right. I agree with that.

INSOO: And when he does cocaine, then that's when he stays out longer, many more days.

BETTY: Right.

INSOO: So it seems like both of you know about this very well, about what happens.

DAVE: Yes, we've gone through it.

BETTY: Too well.

INSOO: So you also have some ideas about what you need to do about that?

Dave: Right.

Creating a Scale

INSOO: How confident are you that you can do this, this time? On a scale of 1 to 10.

DAVE: I'd say a 7 right now. I'd say two weeks ago I was on a 9, now I'm back to about a 7.

INSOO: (To Betty) How about you? How confident are you that he can do this, this time?

BETTY: I don't know. Right now I'm not confident at all. You have to understand I have no trust. I want to trust him, I want to believe in him, I want to support him. I want to but he's given me no reason to.

INSOO: So you are at a 1, would you say?

BETTY: I don't know. Maybe at a 4 because I see that he can do it.

INSOO: You know that he can do it.

BETTY: I think he can. I don't know if he wants to though.

INSOO: He did it for 30 days.

BETTY: That's right. He was a much nicer person, too.

INSOO: So you see a glimpse of what he can be like.

BETTY: Yes.

INSOO: Is that what keeps you hanging in there with Dave?

BETTY: Yes.

INSOO: You imagine. You see some glimmer of what he can be like. (To Dave) So you know how to do that?

DAVE: I'm tying to learn.

INSOO: You know how to do it, it sounds like. You've shown Betty that you can.

DAVE: Right. I was a lot less angry person. I expressed my emotions a lot better. It just seems like the tables turned. She was a lot harder to communicate to and I wanted to communicate and you couldn't shut me up.

BETTY: It was a shock to me. He always wanted to talk, talk, talk and I was like, "Get away." I've got a wall up there so high.

INSOO: Is that wall still up there?

BETTY: It was gradually coming down and then he pulled a couple of stunts.

INSOO: And that's why you are up to 4 in your confidence.

BETTY: Yes.

INSOO: That's a lot. That's a lot for somebody who went through what she went through with you (to Dave).

DAVE: Yes.

INSOO: You said your confidence is about 7 or so. What gives you that much confidence?

DAVE: I think if I lose it this time, lose my family, it's going to be forever. I don't want to go back to how the last four months were. I have my own apartment still, I have a lease on it. It's just a horrible place for me to go. I have bad feelings when I go there. It's a real lonely place. I have a lot of bad memories from that.

INSOO: About the apartment?

DAVE: Right.

INSOO: So you don't want that?

DAVE: No. I went through a period of time where I didn't see my children for probably six weeks. That was real hard.

INSOO: It seems like when you are remembering how bad it is to be in that apartment and how difficult it is for you not to see your children, that's when you do better.

DAVE: I would like to think so. It definitely motivates me a lot more.

INSOO: So what do you have to do to keep remembering that?

DAVE: I always remember it, it's just sometimes there's things that will block it. Like I said, if I hang out with my friends, certain people I hang out with, and they start . . . My mind can be switched to different things pretty fast. I really need to stay away from all that stuff for now until I'm completely out. I won't be drinking or anything anymore.

INSOO: Is there something that Betty and the children can do to be helpful to you so that you can be reminded of that? What can they do to be helpful to you so that you can keep remembering that?

DAVE: I don't think they can do anything. I think it's all got to be myself now. They've done everything they can. I would like a little more confidence from her. That would help. A little bit more support. But I guess she has done that over the years . . . and now, I should have taken advantage of it when she was giving it to me.

Asking, "What Helps?"

INSOO: Suppose she was more supportive, gave you encouragement. What difference is it going to make for you?

DAVE: It would make a lot.

INSOO: How?

DAVE: I think if she didn't drink, that would be a lot more supportive. She doesn't drink around me but she drinks.

INSOO: So her not drinking would be helpful.

DAVE: Right. I don't like it when she drinks either, but she's nothing like I was.

INSOO: So what difference would that make? Her not drinking.

DAVE: It would make a minor, not a whole lot, but it would make somewhat of a difference.

INSOO: Somewhat of a difference?

DAVE: Right. Around me I don't want her drinking at all, but it would make a small difference if she didn't drink. Her drinking doesn't affect me as far as my drinking at least. I would just like a little bit more support, like, "I believe in you." But like I said, she's done that over the past and I've let her down. So a lot of it's on my own time.

INSOO: So her saying that to you would be helpful.

DAVE: Yes.

INSOO: What difference would that make?

DAVE: It would help me believe in myself a little bit more.

INSOO: I see. So you need to believe in yourself more?

DAVE: Right. It's like when I go to AA meetings and the people lend me support. That really helps me believe in myself a lot more.

INSOO: So you can get that from AA. And you're saying getting that from Betty would make more of a difference?

DAVE: Correct.

INSOO: So what do you have to do to get that kind of support from her?

DAVE: Show her that she can believe in me. Prove to her.

INSOO: You have to prove to her. What do you have to do?

DAVE: Just be there all the time and prove that I won't be out drinking and things like that. Give it a little bit of time.

INSOO: I have a lot more to ask you but I realize we are running out of time. (To Betty) Do you have any questions of either Dave or me at this point? Do you have any questions of each other?

BETTY: No.

INSOO: All right. This is the point that I'm going to ask you to step down. We have some seats for you.

The Team's Reactions and Compliments

INSOO: Would the team please come up? Say a little bit about yourselves?

JIM: I'm Jim and I work in the substance abuse counseling program at Hillson County Department of Health.

TERRI: I'm Terri, the clinical supervisor for the same program.

CHARLIE: I'm Charlie. I'm in private practice.

INSOO: It sounds like you are the therapist for this family.

JIM: I've worked primarily with Dave.

TERRI: They haven't done any family therapy yet. We were waiting until after this, and then I'll do the family therapy. We'll do the follow-up if they would like that, if they think that would be helpful.

INSOO: So what's your reaction? What do you think? What strikes you about them?

TERRI: I'm impressed that they're here so early. I know that Betty worked last night. It's really impressive that they are willing to work so hard to be a family. It's so important that they would be here in front of a huge crowd on a Sunday morning to start working toward a solution.

INSOO: Right. That's very positive.

CHARLIE: I'm impressed with that as well, and I'm impressed with the survival ability of the family to go through these ups and downs. Dave is really clear about what he needs to do and what the problem is between friends and family. He seems really drawn toward the family, which is fantastic, and I can understand because they're certainly drawn toward him. And Betty, I was really impressed with her forthrightness and her ability to express her doubts and be really specific about what would be different for her.

INSOO: She seemed very clear about that, the difference between drinking and nondrinking.

JIM: I'm really impressed with the overall commitment to staying together and reaching a solution for each of them. There's a lot of commitment to the whole family that I see with both Dave and Betty. I'm very impressed that they're here and that they were brave enough to come and sit on a stage and do this in front of a group of people. I see a lot of hope.

INSOO: It seemed that even though they have gone through lots of ups and downs over a long period of time, Betty seems to still have this idea that he can do it.

CHARLIE: Yes.

INSOO: She is hanging in there in spite of all her experience telling her otherwise.

CHARLIE: A 4, which is high.

INSOO: Yes. Wow, that's amazing.

TERRI: One of the things I wrote down is I'm real impressed with how wise it is that they're going slow to build a new solid foundation as a family. It's a combination between hanging in there and being wise enough to go slow.

INSOO: At 2. She says her hopes go up and then she gets shot down.

CHARLIE: Kind of a safety factor.

INSOO: So her not trusting at this point makes perfect sense. Maybe that will be helpful for Dave as well. I think he's right, he needs to prove himself that this time it's different.

CHARLIE: One of the differences seems to be that Dave is going to take Antabuse.

INSOO: Yes, his willingness to take Antabuse.

CHARLIE: Which I see as kind of an insurance policy, too.

TERRI: That makes a difference for both.

INSOO: He seems to know that it's the drinking that leads to drugs which leads to being gone for three days, four days. He's very clear about what he has to do. That's a good point.

TERRI: What was also curious is what Dave was doing differently during those nine weeks because he wasn't on Antabuse and he wasn't in jail for all that time. I'm just curious about what he was doing differently to make that change. He said several times that the setback was different, but how did Dave stop? Because he was saying that the alcohol led to the drug use and that he'd drink and it was a setback, but [that time] it didn't lead to drug use. I'm just curious about what was different.

INSOO: He seemed to think it had to do with the friends. When he doesn't hang out with the friends, then it just gets into one day of drinking and doesn't lead to drugs, that's how he seemed to think. How does he manage to stay away from friends?

CHARLIE: Where is he?

INSOO: I don't know. Where does this happen that he stays away from his friends? That's not clear. I should have asked that. That would have been helpful.

JIM: One of the things that I also noticed and was very impressed with about Betty was her ability to say that she was taking care of herself and the kids. Skepticism is one way she is taking care of herself in her situation. I also saw Dave being responsive to that and saying, "She's right. She's absolutely right. She should be skeptical," and being able to own up to some of his own behavior.

CHARLIE: He said, "It's just myself now, it really is up to me to make the change." He's very realistic about that. Sometimes clients, and not only clients but also all of us, come to a clear realization and it's very profound. One of the things Dave said was, "If I don't get on this I'm going to lose my family forever," which I think is an important perspective. It can be very motivating and I don't know if that had to do with him being more interested in taking Antabuse or something, but he mentioned his family over and over again. We know alcohol is a very difficult thing to overcome, but it seemed to me that the family might give him that hope to be able to overcome that.

The Couple's Reaction

INSOO: Okay. We'll ask the couple to come up. What was it like for you, listening?

DAVE: It seems like they hit it right on the head.

INSOO: They have?

DAVE: Yes.

INSOO: They've hit the nail on the head?

BETTY: I agree.

INSOO: You agree. What part? What part was hitting the nail?

DAVE: They just seemed to know our family pretty well by what they heard. My family is very important to me. One question I didn't answer, for the nine weeks I wasn't in jail the whole time, but because I lost my family I was trying to win them back. So I decided to work on myself and was working out and trying to get myself in shape physically, too.

INSOO: You did that in those nine weeks?

DAVE: I tried, yes. Trying to get them back. Getting physically in shape got me mentally in shape, too, so after the 30 days I stayed in the work release program. Best thing that happened to me. She probably wishes I was there still (laughs).

INSOO: What about you, Betty? What was it like for you to listen in on the conversation of the team?

BETTY: I agreed with everything they said and I think it kind of gave me a little bit more hope that they see hope.

INSOO: Any other reactions you have?

DAVE: It made me feel a little bit better, too, that they gave me a little bit of assurance that I could do it. That's why I agreed to come here. I thought it would help me out a little bit more.

INSOO: So you saw this as another approach for you to go in the right direction?

DAVE: Right. Hopefully.

INSOO: So you are going to think about that, right? About how you were able to do this for nine weeks.

DAVE: Right.

INSOO: All by yourself. I should have asked more about that.

DAVE: A lot of it was I wanted to be back with my family and I was real alone without them.

BETTY: I don't know why it's slacked off since he's moved back in.

INSOO: Is that something you wanted to talk to each other about?

BETTY: Yes.

INSOO: So you need some ideas from him about that. Is that something you can do on your own after this meeting today?

BETTY: I don't know. With Jim, right?

DAVE: We were hoping to have some follow-up counseling. It's not just for the alcohol, for the whole family.

INSOO: (To Betty) Are you open for that? Following up with some counseling for the whole family?

BETTY: Yes.

INSOO: Good. So you know what to do?

DAVE: Yes.

INSOO: Okay. Thank you for coming.

DAVE: Thank you very much.

As the couple's reaction to the team's observations indicate, being more hopeful was triggered by the discussion of what was "different" for the couple. Many things are different about Dave's drinking this time, but until Insoo raises the question about what's different the clients do not recognize the difference or define it as meaningful. We emphasize this because without a difference, no matter how small, there is no change.

ONE FINAL CASE STUDY: DREW'S REMARKABLE RESOURCES

Norm was introduced to 10-year-old Drew and his little sister, Tina, by their mother, who explained that although she had divorced the children's alcoholic father several years ago she was still worried about the effects his drinking had on the children, particularly Drew. She was not confident in her ability to help her son and wanted him in therapy with a professional who understood the harmful effects of growing up in an "alcoholic family." Drew also thought this was a good idea. As he explained, both he and his sister continued regular visits with their father. Drew spoke about several incidents, including being hit by his father 2½ years ago, his father's disciplinary lectures, during which he called Drew "stupid," his father's repeatedly embarrassing him in front of his friends, and his taking Tina's side in every dispute, and a persistent fear that his father would unintentionally drive over his pet cat.

Drew was also able to clearly say how he coped with these problems, "I don't talk to my dad when he is drinking, I wait until I'm back with my mom. I talk to her. I get my feelings out in the open." Drew also had a positive experience talking with his school guidance counselor (who was no longer available due to a job change). Although Drew's mom recognized the value of their "talks," she was convinced the real help for Drew was in the hands of a professional.

In the second of only four sessions, Drew came in quite upset. He said he was losing his best friend (his mother) to his little sister's annoying misbehavior. Every time he tried to have a talk with her, his sister would butt in and demand attention. He had even tried to talk with his mom, while his sister was playing outside, only to have her come into the house crying from a fall. Rather than solve this problem for him, Norm asked, "How do you usually solve tough problems like this?" Drew thought for a while and then explained that he first considers what's fair in the situation before taking any action. He then considers what's safe and even if something is fair (like being able to go to the arcade in the mall), if it's not safe (kids his age get into trouble when they are alone in a mall) he'll go with what is safe. Then he added, "I make up my mind and do it." By considering what was fair in this situation, Drew concluded having time alone with his mom was fair. When safety was considered, Drew concluded he didn't want to do anything to hurt his mom's feelings. The problem was, how could he tell his mom he wanted to talk to her alone when he could never find time alone to talk to her (he refused to tell her in front of his little sister because he was concerned that might hurt his mother's feelings)? After brainstorming ways people communicate, Drew decided to write her a letter that he could mail from his dad's house (he thought a letter mailed to his mom from her house would be silly).

The letter worked. Drew began to understand that he could get what he wanted and his mother began to understand that her relationship with her son was his most important and vital resource.

Chapter 10

DWI Offenders

It seems that any discussion of treatment approaches with clients convicted of a drinking and driving offense inevitably includes arguments for and against moderate drinking. Some practitioners believe a DWI (driving while intoxicated) conviction is a sure sign of alcoholism and insist on abstinence-based treatment. Others believe it is foolish to force abstinence on a client population that will return to drinking as soon as their driver's license is reinstated. Many professionals prefer a treatment approach that recognizes the client's use of alcohol and teaches responsible use. Our position recognizes the wisdom of both abstinence and moderate drinking approaches.

DWI OFFENDERS ALREADY KNOW HOW TO DRIVE WITHOUT DRINKING

Every DWI offender has had at least one occasion when he had too much to drink, had the keys to his car, and decided not to drive. On this exceptional occasion, the offender was a nondriving drinker. Our job in therapy is to explore this exception and help our client figure out a way to make this exception the rule. We want to help our client create solutions where he is either a nondrinking driver or a nondriving drinker.

GROUP THERAPY FOR DWI OFFENDERS

After experimenting with both individual and group modalities of doing solution-focused therapy with our DWI Clients, we have decided that solution-focused group therapy produces better results because:

1. Groups generate more exceptions.
2. Groups generate more "how to" ideas.
3. Groups help clients believe in their own expertise.
4. Group members listen to and learn from each other more readily than from a "know it all" expert.

Questions from the Field:

"Does this approach conform to state laws?"

In most states, most treatment programs are required to follow the guidelines and assessment established by the state. This particular program, developed by Norm for first offenders, conforms to Vermont state requirements.

Ten Sessions

You may follow the group therapy format we outline here or adapt parts of it to fit your needs. We use a 10-week format because it conforms with the treatment requirements in Vermont. We also have rolling admissions into the group. Rolling admissions meets two needs: the need of the client to have his license returned in a timely manner and the need of the program to meet access standards.

During the initial interview most DWI Clients have only one working goal: "I want to get my driver's license back." While we sympathize with the client's thinking, it will not earn the approval of the state authorities who referr these cases to us. These authorities want these troublesome drivers to understand that it is their drinking that caused the DWI conviction. They also want the clients to make some significant changes in how, when, where, and how much alcohol they use. To resolve this difference between where our clients are and where the state authorities want them to be, we use the substance user's competency checklist and worksheet (see appendix) as a group session tool. After the client completes this form his goals will not only be more acceptable to the state authorities, they will also be tailored to his situation. Following are guidelines for using the checklist and worksheet with a group.

1. We explain to our clients that the return of their driver's license is only one of the goals of our treatment group. We also want to help them make some changes so that they do not get another DWI.

2. We then instruct our clients to turn to the form. We point out that there are five sections and each section contains questions accompanied by a rating scale that runs from "never" to "always" with five numerical *shades of gray* in between. We ask the group members to rate each item with a checkmark on the corresponding scale. We usually use item 7 of the second section as an example. We state that it reads, "I participate in regular exercise," and continue with, "If you have never considered regular exercise, then check 'never.' If, however, you are currently exercising regularly, check 'always.' If you are somewhere in between, check the

• •

Questions from the Field:

"Don't clients complain that the solution-focused approach is mechanical?"

We can understand how someone might get that impression—our strategies are rigorous and the phrasing of questions is precise. However, that may be more of a therapist's impression than our client's. Norm recently received this unsolicited feedback:

> *"Thanks to your efforts, I have recently reacquired my license, after completing your DWI counseling course. I have never felt comfortable with psychology or psychologists, because I've always felt (and still do) that this field is more of an art than a science. Having said that, I'd like you to know that I think you're one hell of an artist. Keep up the good work and thanks again. If I can be of service to your groups in the future, either for testimonials or as an example of what not to do behind the wheel, please feel free to contact me."*

number that best reflects the amount of exercise you do."

3. We have a supply of pencils and pens ready. After the instructions are understood by everyone, we give them ample time to fill out the checklist and ask them to pause before going to the worksheet.

4. When everyone is finished with the checklist, we instruct them to turn their attention to the goal worksheet. The first part of the worksheet asks for a decision; the second part asks for an explanation. You may want to give explicit instructions such as, "To make your goals unique to your life, we need to know what you can work on in this program that will make a difference." We then instruct the group to choose from the checklist which items will make a difference when "just a little" improvement is made. We again use the example of regular exercise to illustrate our instructions.

5. We have found that it is worth repeating to our clients that they enrolled in a *drinking driver rehabilitation* program and as such their goals must have something to do with their use of alcohol. But we cannot possibly read their minds and know how making improvements in the areas they have indicated is going to alter their use of alcohol, so they have to tell us. In the final section of the worksheet, they need to explain how improvements in the areas they have selected will make a difference in their use of alcohol.

6. Once all the written work is completed, we ask for volunteers to share the items they have chosen and the explanation of how improvement will make a difference in their drinking. In any group, clients will have common items and ideas about improvement, and a lively discussion can ensue.

7. We always conclude this group session with compliments about our clients' excellent level of participation and ask that they observe what they do to begin making the improvements we have discussed. We also tell them that part of each future session will be a "check in" on the progress they are making.

The group sessions all share the same format: Each week we present a different worksheet (see weekly worksheets in the appendix), give a brief set of instructions, and allow ample time for each client to complete the worksheet. Each of the worksheets asks the same question in a different way: What is already working to reduce your risk of a future DWI conviction? We have found that it does not make a difference which worksheet a client does first, second, third, and so on, so we put them in a random order, following the same sequence that repeats every 10 weeks. We may discard any worksheet on a particular week and ask the nightmare question (see chapters 2 and 13) when we think the group is not fully appreciating the seriousness of a drinking driver conviction and can benefit from a negative vision of the future if changes are not made today.

Each week, when all the clients have completed the worksheet we lead a group discussion by

- soliciting answers from each group member;
- writing the answers down on newsprint;

- facilitating discussion between clients with similar ideas; and
- providing educational comments when appropriate (such as how to calculate a blood alcohol count).

BETWEEN SESSIONS: MORE TALK ABOUT THE PROBLEM

Occasionally we miss a clue and we discover a client's drinking problem is much worse than we thought. Because we are open to hearing our clients' ideas, no matter how outrageous they may sound, clients will tell us when they are having additional problems. For example, when a group discussion leads to a homework assignment focused on the moderate use of alcohol in a social setting and a particular client is not able to do this, he may report his failure to the group. One client in this situation reported that his wife insisted he confess to the group about a beer drinking binge, when he drove from bar to bar. When these difficulties are brought to the group and cannot be resolved within the group, the client is invited to an individual session with the group leader. In the individual sessions we continue to follow a solution-focused approach, asking for a working goal, exceptions, miracles, nightmares, and a working solution. We will also pursue our client's family members as resources to help out with the solution. When additional treatment resources are necessary, we make the appropriate referrals. When we act quickly we find we are able to remain within the framework of our client's original goal: "I want my driver's license back."

• •

Questions from the Field:

I have a hard time getting my mandated DWI clients to talk. It sounds like you get your clients talking. How do you do it?"

We think our clients find it easy to talk in our DWI group because the ideas they are talking about are their own. We don't ask them what they think about some expert's ideas or discuss how they should be ashamed of themselves for getting a DWI. We never try to rub their noses in their mistake. We help them move on and learn what they already know about preventing another mistake. We stimulate clients' thinking with each worksheet and then talk about it. It's easier to talk about something when we give them a few minutes to think it over and write their ideas down. Some clients read from the worksheet, which is their way of talking, and that's okay with us. I guess we just make it easy to talk and then give them compliments for doing it.

COMPLIMENTS AND PAPERWORK

Prior to his final session we review each client's worksheets* to prepare a complimentary summary statement. These statements tie together his goals from the goal worksheet and the comments he has made throughout the

*By the time a client completes the DWI program he will have written and talked about his successful strategies to reduce his risk of reoffense ten times. Immediately after the final interview we photocopy the client's worksheets, store them in a tickler file, and send them to him in six months. A cover letter accompanies this surprise package, asking him to take five minutes to review his hard work.

course. Compliments are given both verbally and in writing on a certificate of program completion (forwarded to the state authority). As a token of our confidence in their ability to remain a nondrinking driver we award all our clients a DON'T DRINK AND DRIVE key fob. We also share our outcome statistics: 2 percent rearrest rate at 1.5 years follow-up. We jokingly ask them to continue to make us look good with their hard work.

• •

Quick Tip:

Figure Out What Does Work

Sometimes when something in the client's life is broken, it cannot be quickly or easily fixed. Usually we encourage the client simply to ignore this so together we can figure out what does work. Then we support the client so she can do that.

Chapter 11
Mandated Clients

Solution-focused therapy is built on constructivism, the philosophical position that asserts reality is quite arbitrary and made up of socially agreed upon values and beliefs. When working with a mandated client we are often asked to consider two different realities: the reality of the person making the referral and the reality presented by the client. When two realities collide, neither is right or wrong. Here is a story-riddle to illustrate our constructivist thinking.

SPEAKER ONE: If a tree falls in a forest does it make a sound?

SPEAKER TWO: No.

SPEAKER ONE: If a tree falls in the forest and there is someone in the forest, does it make a sound?

SPEAKER TWO: Does the person in the forest know the sound of a falling tree and identify this sound as the sound of a falling tree?

SPEAKER ONE: Yes.

SPEAKER TWO: Then yes, the falling tree makes a sound.

SPEAKER ONE: And if she does not know this to be the sound of a falling tree?

SPEAKER TWO: Then the falling tree makes no sound. However, let me ask you, if an airline pilot happened to be hiking in the woods and heard the sound and identified it as the sound of a sonic boom, a sound that is familiar to him, does the falling tree make a sound?

SPEAKER ONE: I do not think so. I think an overhead aircraft has made the sound of a sonic boom.

SPEAKER TWO: Correct. You are understanding reality. And if the hiking pilot happens upon the woman who is also in the woods and who has heard a tree fall, what is the sound that has been made?

SPEAKER ONE: When she is able to convince him the sound was that of a tree falling, then it was a falling tree. If, however, he is more persuasive, then an overhead aircraft has made a sonic boom.

SPEAKER TWO: You are correct again. With two or more people, reality becomes a creation of the social interaction.

Quick Tip:

Therapeutic Leadership

To get the cooperation of your clients, "lead them from one step behind" (Cantwell & Holmes, 1994). Occasionally give them a "tap on the shoulder" with your curiosity and "not knowing" (Anderson & Goolishan, 1992) questions.

When we begin therapy with a client, the reality we talk about is our client's reality. When a client comes to us and complains about a crippling fear every time she hears a loud noise, and she attributes the onset of this crippling fear to a time she was walking in the woods and was frightened by a sonic boom, we agree with her. We confirm her diagnosis of crippling fear that started with a sonic boom. Then we begin to cocreate a new reality by asking, "Are there times when you hear loud noises and are not crippled with fear?" We do not challenge the client's creation of a problem reality, we simply invite her to experience a solution reality, a reality where the problem does not exist.

Imagine for a moment that this woman with the crippling fear brought about by a sonic boom is brought to therapy by her lumberjack husband, a man accustomed to loud noises. He thinks anyone frightened by loud noises is crazy and needs psychiatric help. When asked if she agrees with her husband, she refuses psychiatric help, contending anyone with her experiences would also be frightened. She insists her fear is normal and a helpful defense against possible harm from things that make loud noises. Her only reason for coming to the therapy session is to get him off her back. In this instance each individual in this relationship has created a different reality about reactions to loud noises and has been unsuccessful in influencing the other to come over to his or her side. We would be making a mistake if we were to side with either loud noise reality. Taking sides may provide a temporary truce in the conflict but it does not provide a lasting peace. Our job is to cocreate with both clients a different reality where the problem does not exist. We do this by searching for exceptions to their loud noise reality *conflict*:

1. "Can you tell me about the times you have had similar disagreements and have been able to resolve the disagreement?"

2. "On a scale of 1 to 10 where 1 represents that time when the two of you were the most divided you have ever been on this matter and 10 is a time when this matter no longer concerns either of you, where would you say you are now?" If the number is more than 1 ask, "How have you done that?" When the number is 1 ask, "How are you coping—you know, getting along in spite of this difference?"

When this search for exceptions is successful (and it usually is because the questions themselves create the possibility of a nonproblem reality), we have introduced a new reality the couple can choose to agree upon.

Mandated clients and the people who bring them to therapy often have a relationship similar to the lumberjack and his wife's. Like this woman, mandated alcoholics have ideas that make up their reality. They also have ideas about the reason why they have been brought to therapy and about the people who have accompanied them. While the people who bring us these clients have ideas that make up a problem reality, the clients often disagree, asserting that anyone who shared their life experiences would also drink.

Mandated clients insist their drinking is normal and a useful way to have fun and relax. They would be happy if people would just get off their back.

There is a temptation when working with the mandated client to take sides. Clinicians often think that common sense insists they point out the harm that drinking alcohol has done to the client and side with the person making the referral. To do this would be a mistake. Taking sides alienates the client: The client becomes even less cooperative, thinking the clinician does not understand and support his reality. By taking sides, a clinician can easily turn a mandated client into a mandated and noncompliant client.

We believe a better course of action is to search for any exception to the opposing realities that may lead to a common workable goal for therapy. This search for exceptions can begin with a scaling, such as, "Give me an idea of where the two of you are now on a 1-to-10 scale, where 1 represents that time in your relationship when you were most divided on this drinking problem and 10 is a time when the two of you have resolved this matter. Where are you on this scale now?" When we start our search for exceptions with a scaling question, the following conversation is typical.

SPOUSE: We're not at 1. When we talked last week he did agree to come and see you today.

MANDATED CLIENT: See, this is what I mean. Give her an inch and she'll take your whole foot. (We love the way people mix metaphors and create a phrase that really does capture the essence of their thoughts and feelings.) I didn't agree that I'm some damn alcoholic. I said I'd come here if it would shut you up.

SPOUSE: (Almost crying) This is what I get when I try to help.

THERAPIST: I'm glad the two of you came today. I can understand this is hard on both of you. Okay, you're not at 1. Where would you say you are?

SPOUSE: (Still almost crying), 2 or 3, but he'll say we're at 1.

MANDATED CLIENT: There she goes again, always thinking the worst of me.

THERAPIST: (To the mandated client) Where would you say the two of you are on the scale?

● ●

Questions from the Field:

"How do you deal with the mandated client who tells you some completely unbelievable cock-and-bull story?"

We also have heard these stories. Our clients will come up with the most outrageous stories about how they are clean and sober and it was no effort at all. These stories are just unbelievable. In the traditional model of treatment the therapist would be told, "You must confront that so-and-so." Therapists were told it was a good idea to almost beat the truth out of these clients. Obviously we disagree. In our model we confront these outrageous stories with questions like, "How do you know it was so easy to quit just like that (snap fingers)?" "What does (your wife, probation officer) see that tells her it was that easy for you to quit?" "What will it take for you to continue these changes?" "In three months what will we be able to notice that is different about your life for having made these changes?" Effective, lasting change is always present in the details. When a client gives us an unbelievable story we ask for details. For the most part these cock-and-bull stories make for interesting tales from the trenches, but they are very few in number.

By staying neutral in our search for exceptions we have learned we can ignore the couple's attempts to bait each other and us into taking sides. Our focus is on looking for the progress the couple has already made, no matter how small, in resolving this difficult and painful situation. We have also learned that assuring the couple that we realize how difficult this is for them helps reduce some of the intensity of their fighting.

Once an exception has been established we immediately try to build it into a solution. We do this by asking, "How did you do it, move from 1 all the way up to 2 or 3?" Once we have the specific information on how this couple creates solutions to this difficult disagreement, we invite them to do more of what is already working. When couples like this fall back into quarreling about the drinking problem, they usually turn to the therapist and solicit an expert opinion. In this circumstance we suggest you say, "I'll get right back to that. First I'd like to hear about other ways the two of you solve your problems. Who is usually most invested in getting a problem solved?" "On a scale of 1 to 10, 10 stands for you are willing to do just about anything to solve this problem and 1 stands for you are not about to lift a finger, where would you say you are today?" As soon as we have an answer to this question we again begin creating a solution by asking, "How does that help?" By making a general statement about problem solving that implies this couple can do it, you get yourself out of a sticky situation and put the focus of the session where it belongs—on the couple. By asking the specific question about problem solving and asking a how follow-up question, you have continued to cocreate a solution reality.

CLIENTS ON PROBATION: AN INVOLUNTARY MARRIAGE?

Another common way mandated clients arrive in our office is with a court order that is being enforced by a probation officer. It can be helpful to think about this mandated client more as a couple than as an individual. Similar to bygone days when marriages were arranged and the couple had no option but to learn how to get along with each other, the "marriage" of a probation officer to our mandated client has been arranged by the court and they have no option but to get along with each other or the client risks being sent to jail. Mandated clients are often at odds with their probation officer; each has a different idea about the problem reality. It is helpful to see this clash of realities as just a problem of perception, not a right or wrong way. Working with a mandated client is similar to working with a husband and wife: It is important not to take sides. The first job is to define the goal of therapy, which is best done through questions that ask for a negotiation of the goal by focusing on the idea of a workable solution. Probation officers have come to expect us to ask, "What is the minimum amount of change that is

---

• • • • • • • • • • • • • • • • • •

Quick Tip:

Utilize Change

Change is inevitable. Our therapeutic task is to utilize the changes clients create in the most positive way possible.

acceptable?" and "What will you see about Todd three months from now that will tell you his therapy is working?" This gives the client, and us, some idea of the direction the probation officer is looking for. We follow up these questions with, "What will let you know Todd is working as hard as he can?" and "What will Todd notice about you when he is working as hard as he can?" These follow-up questions open the door to meaningful discussion about workable solutions. For instance, if the goal is to stop drinking, and the probation officer will know Todd is headed in the right direction when he goes to Alcoholics Anonymous meetings, we then turn to Todd and ask him how ready he is to take the first small step, how he knows he is ready, and what his first small step will be. We also like to ask our clients what they will be doing when their probation officer notices positive changes. Once we get things going in a positive direction we like to provide optimistic support that these changes can continue. Optimism seems like an important ingredient for both the probation officer and our client, perhaps because in their world there is so much failure that optimism is hard to come by.

• •

Questions from the Field:

"What do you do when you find out your client is lying to you?"

Yes, this does happen when clients are forced to be in therapy. Particularly so when there is a another person pushing the client and we are brought in to "shape him up." They usually want us to give the client a stern lecture or a warning that bad behavior will simply not be tolerated. Sometimes these people want us to kick a client out of our program as a way to teach them a lesson. We do not like it when clients try to pull the wool over our eyes but we do not believe that harsh treatment of any kind is effective. We simply do not see how a harsh approach helps the client. We prefer to look at the issue of lying from a different angle. We ask the client how conflicting stories, between himself and his probation officer for instance, could possibly be helpful. We encourage the client to share his hopeful expectation of what he wanted to happen by lying to us. Most clients have the expectation that by lying (usually about their substance use) they will get out of therapy with a good recommendation from us. When we know the client wants a good recommendation from us (or from the person doing the pushing), we can explore ways other than lying that will get them what they really want. Of course, this leads us to a discussion of positive changes that the client will have to carry out.

Chapter 12
Group Therapy

Working with clients in groups has always been and will always be the major modality of treatment for substance abuse problems. Working with groups allows treatment to be accessible, economical, and effective. However, traditional substance abuse treatment groups have one major drawback: Participants are forced to adhere to the philosophical viewpoint of the facility before they can be viewed as making progress. Initial treatment plans from these facilities often start with goals that include the personal acceptance of the disease concept of addiction and acceptance of the first three steps of Alcoholics Anonymous. Treatment groups are used to pressure newcomers into accepting this treatment plan by seasoned members of the community. We have not found these methods to be helpful, especially when the client has a different idea about his drinking problem. Rather than format our groups around indoctrination into a single model of addiction and recovery, we format our groups with the same solution focus we use when working with individuals. For the most part, clients select one of our groups based upon the focus of the group. For example, clients hoping to solve codependency problems attend our codependency group; clients who want support in their recovery will choose our ongoing support group. When clients select groups in this manner, they are in effect telling us in advance what problem they want to work on, therefore, in group we resist problem talk and immediately focus on exceptions to the problem. When we focus on exceptions we quickly discover the advantages of having many minds: Many different viewpoints build many different solutions.

There are two ways to conduct groups. One has all members begin on the same date and end at a specific date several weeks later. This model works well for practices and clinics that have a large pool of potential participants and enough groups with staggered starting dates to guarantee good client access. While many therapists prefer to work with groups that are time-limited and have a definite beginning, middle, and end phase, the second type of group, sometimes called a rolling admission group, is more practical for a small, or medium-sized practice or clinic. In this format the client's participation is limited to a specific time period but the group itself is ongoing. Immediate access is the obvious advantage to rolling admission groups. Clients do not have to wait weeks before the next group begins. This format strikes us as reasonable and realistic because it resembles how life is really like. No one we know has all the same friends they knew in childhood; it is normal to drop and add friends throughout our lives. Families are not created in an instant with grandparents, parents, and children all coming on board at the same time. We are all in different stages of different kinds of relationships with a variety of people. We prefer our treatment groups to be as close to clients' real life situations as possible. We know that when they build solutions within the diversity of our groups, they can also build solutions within the diversity of their lives. We also prefer a heterogeneous group within a reasonable limit (abusers and victims may not work well together, for instance) because ideas for solutions can come from many surprising places, teaching group members to take advantage of new ideas for solutions.

KITCHEN TABLE SOLUTIONS

There are times when we become so insulated in our work and so far removed from real life that we want to shake our heads and laugh. The simple matter of a table in the group room is one of these times. In traditional psychodynamic psychotherapy, the idea of a group of clients sitting around a table is abhorrent. We can hear them saying, "These people spend their lives putting barriers between themselves and other people—no tables in my group!" But think about where most people tackle the difficult problems they face: over a cup of coffee at a kitchen table! So if regular people tackle a problem with a table between them, it made sense to us to experiment with tables in our therapy groups. Our client satisfaction surveys indicate our clients prefer the "round table" groups. Far from being a barrier between people, we have seen a tabletop become a conduit that connects people. A table is also a convenient place to rest a cup of coffee and to fill out checklists and weekly worksheets!

LARGE GROUPS

Ben Furman of Helsinki, Finland, calls his work with large psychiatric groups "laziness therapy" (personal communication, 1996). He has the large group break up into small groups of two or three. He then tosses out a solution-focused question for the clients to work on while he sits back sipping tea and acting lazy. Norm uses this same approach with his large recovery support group, but sees himself as clever and hard working. After breaking the group into small groups of two or three, he asks them a solution-focused question about their week, such as, "What have you done this week to make your life better?" "What would your (friends, family, coworkers) say they notice that tells them you are a new person?" or " When were you tempted to handle something the same old way and said to yourself, 'No, I'm going to handle it differently this time'?" Of course, not every client has an outstanding story of success to tell every week, but enough have something to say that a lively discussion gets going. After the small groups have had a good chance to talk the question over, Norm gets the larger group back together to share some summarizing stories and compliments.

DECENTRALIZED POWER

Sometimes what we do accidentally is more powerful than what we do on purpose. Some years ago Norm took a two-week, long-deserved vacation. When he returned to work, the clinic's office manager pulled him aside to compliment him on the good behavior of his alcohol recovery group. At the time the clinic did not have a group room and Norm met with his clients in the employee kitchen. When Norm left for his vacation he forgot to tell his group they would not be meeting for two weeks. When they showed up the

first week, they met without him and decided to meet without him the second week. On each occasion they fixed coffee as was the group custom and cleaned up after themselves. The office manager could not believe a group of alcoholics could take responsibility for themselves. Since this first accidental leaderless group, we have designed all our groups to function when we are not present. This decentralization of the expert power is a cornerstone of solution-focused therapy and to carry it over into the structure of our groups makes sense. Our clients have reported some lively discussions in our absence and have all learned how to ask for exceptions and use scaling questions with each other.

• •

Questions from the Field:

"What about in-home detox?"

We hate to admit this, but Norm has been around long enough to remember the old days *of alcohol treatment. Before we got fancy with medically monitored detox, when an alcoholic started to go into difficult withdrawal we gave him a small shot of booze. That was in-home detox. Currently, many clinics that follow a solution-focused therapy approach use an in-home detox. Protocols usually include daily contact with a medical professional for a vital signs check-in and, when necessary for serious withdrawal symptoms, a small dose of a benzodiazapine. We recommend coordinating these daily check-ins with a visit with a counselor for moral support and solution building. It is important to build upon what is already working during the first few days of recovery. We suggest the counselor focus on what's working rather than review a daily problem list. This approach is not only more positive but also can give hope to the client that solutions to his drinking problem are indeed happening.*

A GOOD GAME FOR "NOT SO TALKATIVE" GROUPS

We have all encountered a group that is difficult to get talking; no matter how we phrase a question it seems to fall flat. In these situations we suggest you try playing a game with the group members. The following list of questions is a game we play with a pair of dice. Each client takes a turn rolling the dice. She then must answer the question from the list of competency questions below that corresponds to the total of the roll of her dice. Either the group leader or the client picks the category of question: individual, family, or general focus. Therapists can use their intuition to formulate a few follow-up questions to ask the client after she has answered the initial question. These follow-up questions can help the client clarify her answer and personalize it to her goal.

Competency Questions

Individual Focus

Doubles   What's better today and how did you accomplish it?

Two   Who, other than yourself, has noticed the improvements you have made, and what have they noticed?

Three   How do you explain the changes you have been able to make?

Four   What needs to happen (even today) so you can say, "Recovery is a good idea"?

Five   When are you now most able to refuse a drink or drug, and how do you do that? Also, when are you least able to refuse a drink or drug, and how do you do that?

Six   What's the simplest and easiest thing you can do to keep your recovery going?

Seven   How has your not drinking (or drugging) helped you?

Eight   How do you know this is a good time to be starting your recovery?

Nine   What would you say you have done that explains the progress you have made?

Ten   What will you be doing when your problems with alcohol and drugs are no longer a focus in your life?

Eleven   Suppose you decide to do even more of what you have discovered works, what will you be doing in three months that you are not doing now?

Twelve   What will you do today to keep your recovery going?

Family Focus

Doubles   How does your family explain the progress you've made?

Two   When do you want your family to help you? How will they know you want their help?

Three   What will be happening that will let your family know you are on the right track with your recovery?

Four   What will your family notice is different about you in 3, 6, 9 months?

Five   How will the changes you are making help your family?

Six   What is the minimum amount of change your family will accept?

Seven   Suppose a miracle happens for you and your family, what difference would a miracle make?

Eight	How does your family know you are committed to making changes?
Nine	Since your recovery started, what was the best day? How did you and your family do that?
Ten	How did your family know this was a good time for you to start your recovery?
Eleven	Who in your family usually gets you into action?
Twelve	Who in your family has solved a drinking problem, and how did he or she do it?

General Focus

Doubles	Where will you be next year, and what will you be doing that is better than what you are doing now?
Two	How are you treated differently when you are sober?
Three	How will making these positive changes affect your life?
Four	Who has been most helpful to you in your attempts to manage your life?
Five	What do other people know about you that gives them the confidence that you will succeed?
Six	How well have the changes you have made worked?
Seven	What is already working in your life?
Eight	What have you done this week to make your life better?
Nine	When were you tempted to handle something the same old way and you said, "No, I'm going to handle this differently"? What did you do?
Ten	What are the three most valuable assets you have? How do you use them to your advantage?
Eleven	What kind of help do people need from you so they can communicate better with you?
Twelve	What would your family say they would like to see you keep doing that is helpful to them?

USING THE NIGHTMARE QUESTION WITH A MANDATED GROUP

The nightmare question does not always work with mandated clients. The mandated client is usually only participating in therapy to please a parent, spouse, or other family member or to avoid legal consequences. The mandated client's nightmare vision is limited to the enforcement of the negative consequences inherent in his failure to comply with the demands of therapy; they are prepared to do whatever the therapist suggests, at least until he has *done his time* and is let *off the hook*.

When working with a mandated client who has been convicted of a first offense for driving while intoxicated, you can capitalize on the client's willingness to participate in almost anything and insist he explore a nightmare day as part of group treatment. In one such group, each of three clients agreed their nightmare day would be to wake up to the realization that they had become hard core alcoholics. One client added that he would have killed someone while driving in a blackout. When asked how they would feel on this nightmare morning, their list of feelings included anger, disappointment, confusion, despair, shame, and depression. Further discussion focused on their unanimous amazement that they would have let their drinking get so bad. One client summarized the group's feeling by saying, "I would feel ashamed to allow myself to get that way."

As we continued to explore the consequences by asking who else would notice they were living a nightmare day, responses ranged from everyone who read the newspaper headlines of a DWI fatality to friends, family, and coworkers. The most noticeable features people would notice included lack of motivation, bad attitude, loss of interest, and despair. With the nightmare day developed in this manner, we concluded by asking if there were warning signs that this nightmare was on the horizon. Again the group was unanimous in their opinion that they did not see any of this nightmare happening to them. We persisted by simply asking, "Are you sure?" One client conceded that this DWI conviction and all the inconvenience it has caused him could be understood as a "wake-up call." As he put it, "I don't see it ever happening, but if I hadn't been stopped now, it (drinking) could have gone on to get worse." With this admission the group joined in a discussion of how they were each responsible for their arrest and conviction (instead of blaming the timing, circumstances, police, and judicial system) and the changes each must make to lower their risk for future drinking problems. On occasions like this, when the nightmare question has worked with mandated clients, seeing a negative picture of the future allows them to understand they will have a drinking problem later if they do not take the opportunity to make some changes *now*.

GROUPS FOR FAMILIES

Many therapists who work with individuals seem reluctant to venture into expanding their practice to include couples and families. By the same token, many family therapists seem reluctant to expand their practice to include group work, particularly multifamily groups. In Vermont, those of us interested in innovation and family therapy were fortunate to learn from the pioneering work of the late Spike Almy and his family groups at the Vermont State Hospital. In an environment that could easily have been described as a holding cell for society's unwanted chronically mentally ill, Spike turned "visiting day" into a therapeutic opportunity, using multiple-family therapy groups as the vehicle to transport patients and their families from their despair to a hopeful future. The mythology that has grown over the years about Spike's heroic work often inspires us to do bold things with our challenging families.

The following exercise was designed to be used in a multifamily group to

• • • • • • • • • • • • • • • • • • • •

Quick Tip:

About Change

Changes come from many sources and directions. Living changes us everyday.

help families maintain the positive changes that they have begun both on their own and in individual and group therapy.

1. In a single-session multiple-family group, present a few desirable characteristics of recovery (family activity, doing chores together, fewer arguments).

2. Ask the group to brainstorm a complete list from their own experiences, expectations, and hopes. Allow ample time for this activity.

3. Ask the group to separate into families and to choose two or three items that would make a big difference if they were to follow through their ideas.

4. Gather the families back into a large group and ask families to report their short list of items for improvement. Record these on newsprint.

5. They then return to their family work groups to discuss what each would notice that would tell him or her the family was moving in a positive direction.

6. Ask them to again return to the large group to report these imagined observations. Record these on newsprint.

7. Begin a large group discussion of each family's decision-making process. Ask the general question, "How did your family go about deciding which three items from the large list were the important items for you?" followed by, "How is this different from the way you would have made a family decision before starting our recovery program?" These two questions are usually enough to get members from one family talking to members of other families. A lively discussion develops.

8. Ask the families to quickly get back together; conclude the session by asking each family to decide and report back (from where they are seated) what each member must do to keep the positive changes going over the next few weeks.

In the course of this exercise we summarize items each family chooses for improvement, the dysfunctional methods each family has used in the past, and the wide variety of new behaviors many of the family members are currently using. However, we refrain from using negative labels to describe any of the behaviors family members talk about; we reframe in a positive light any behaviors that are described with a negative label.

••

Chapter 13

When Substance Abuse Is a Problem Among Problems

CLIENTS WITH A DUAL DIAGNOSIS

At times we encounter reluctance from the mental health community to treating people with substance abuse problems and reluctance from the substance abuse treatment community to treating people with mental health problems. "I don't know enough about depression, anxiety, or posttraumatic stress disorder; how can I possibly work with these diagnoses?" We understand the "turf" issues involved in treating each other's clients when an agency's livelihood is at stake. We also understand that professionals are afraid of making a mistake with each other's clients because they have been taught that only an expert knows how to work with certain clients. The expert's way is to use the problem-solving approach. The problem-solving approach insists the therapist's first job is to make an accurate diagnosis so the appropriate treatment plan can be given to the client. The problem-solving approach has spawned a cadre of experts for each *DSM-IV* diagnosis who can prescribe exact treatments until the cows come home. Some of these treatments that come with the expert's blessing actually work, but not because the diagnosis and treatment are such a good match (as the experts think); any treatment will work for some of the people some of the time simply because people are so similar in the way they work at building solutions to their serious problems. Even the most haphazardly prescribed treatment plan will work occasionally. We believe the most valuable resource in helping people make changes in their life is not a diagnostic manual or a library of "what works" books written by experts, but the client sitting right in front of you.

In our view, a natural way of working with people in a substance abuse setting who have mental health problems (and vice versa) is to forget about the diagnosis and work directly with the client and her family. You can use the protocol we proposed for working with the chronic relapsing client (see chapter 8) when working with the dually diagnosed client. The cornerstone of success is early involvement of supportive people and family members, and continued use of their skills as often as is possible.

In therapy the therapist can help her client discover times when she does something to make her life better in spite of the problem. When working with the dual diagnosis client we suggest the therapist use the same strategies as previously detailed in this book. Start with questions about pre-session change. Continue with questions about coping with the problem and what the client has done to keep the problem from getting worse. Ask the miracle question with dogged curiosity, refusing to give up when the client says, "I don't know" or "Oh, a miracle could never happen to someone like me." When this happens either sit silently as a signal to your client that you have not yet heard an answer or tell your client, "Take a guess. What might a miracle look like in your life?" Finally, use scales to help your client conceptualize what the next small step will look like. By the end of the session you will have developed a workable solution without the benefit of either a diagnosis or the expert's blessing.

• •

Questions from the Field:

"What about underlying causes? You don't seem to pay much attention to them."

In his movie Chalk Talk on Alcoholism, *Father Martin (1992) describes two very different rationalizations for substance abuse. In the first instance he exposes the common man's rationalizations with the long string of drinking days, "Birthdays, holidays, holy days, fast days, Sundays, Mondays, Tuesdays, Wednesdays . . ." We get the point: The reasons the common man gives for his drinking have nothing to do with his drinking problem. Father Martin continues by exposing the intelligent man's rationalizations with another string, "tension, frustration, anxiety, jobs . . ." Father Martin asserts, "Knowing why he drinks does not stop an alcoholic from drinking." Father Martin, as Steve de Shazer would say, had a way of "getting to the surface of the problem." We also agree with an AA saying, "I have met many a man too smart to get sober, but never one too dumb." In our view, underlying causes may exist with a drinking problem but they are not the cause of the drinking problem. These underlying causes are just another problem we address with the solutions we build with our clients. We have found that when effective solutions to the substance abuse problems are implemented, most of the underlying problems are no longer a problem.*

GROUP THERAPY

In addition to individual therapy we encourage therapists working with dual diagnosed clients to form a therapy group. Group therapy offers the following advantages:

1. It provides a place for people to gather with others who are experiencing similar problems.

2. It offers a place to validate, through conversations with peers, life experiences they only know to be true from their private reflections about what is happening to them.

3. It gives clients the opportunity to gain better control of their life through group solution building. This can make a significant contribution to building positive self-esteem.

4. It gives clients the opportunity to share their life story without molding it to fit the confines of a more restrictive group (for example, in AA one is supposed to talk only about alcohol).

Finally, group therapy provides a "laboratory" for therapists working with this special treatment situation. These clients are experts at managing very difficult life circumstances. The synergy of a therapy group allows the therapist to learn more about what works than will any amount of careful listening in individual sessions. In a therapy group, clients can weigh each other's ideas about many helpful topics, including effective tools for each problem, how to manage solutions that work for one problem but may make the other problem worse, how to effectively cope with medications and their side effects, how to know when a therapy (psychotherapy or medication therapy) is not working and how to effectively use resources.

•••

Questions from the Field:

"Do you talk to your clients about medication and its side effects?"

Neither of us are medical doctors so we are not qualified or licensed to give advice about medication. This does not, however, stop many in the field of substance abuse from giving out free advice. We have spoken with clients who return from an AA meeting completely confused because someone acting as an expert told him that he would never be sober until he get off his medication.

In our approach we try to remember the adage, "When you give a man a fish you feed him for the day; when you teach a man to fish you feed him for a lifetime." When we work with a client who has a question about his medication or its side effects, we use a solution-focused approach and consult his expertise on the matter with questions like, "How have you gotten medication questions answered in the past?" When a client is in control of the information he needs to be able to make an intelligent decision, we believe he is in better control of his life. When we are able to help a client get his own answers to his nagging questions, we believe we have opened the door to a lifetime of better self-control.

CRISIS INTERVENTION

One major focus of our work with dual diagnosed clients is the prevention of repeated hospitalizations and rehabs. When some clients fall, they seem to fall really hard. This will often present as a crisis and give the appearance that all we have gained in therapy is totally lost. This is not the case. Instead of hospitalizing the client we remind him that he has been in these crisis situations before and has gotten out of them by doing something for himself. We suggest you ask your client questions like, "What are you forgetting to do?" "What did you do the last time that helped you get back on an even keel?" Even when the client wants to go into the hospital, first ask, "How is the hospital going to help you?" and follow the question with, "How else can you get that same thing?" We believe diverting dual diagnosed clients away from hospital and rehab stays is important to building their sense of independence and success. Once they learn that they can do something to help themselves, they reduce their reliance on the "expert" medical professionals to fix their life for them.

WORKING WITH CLIENTS ON MEDICATION

This is a frequently asked question from those who believe that we oppose medication in general. We observe that most substance abusers are essentially "self-medicators" and they seem to know the physiological changes that medication can cause better that we can possibly tell them. But then, today the population as a whole might be described the same way.

We become concerned, however, when clients view medication as the solution to the problems of life and their role as a passive recipient of the benefits of what the medicine has to offer. In order to keep them viewing their efforts as an active participant in getting healthier and better, we frequently ask the following questions while we are monitoring the medications:

- What are you doing to help the medication work for you?
- What are you willing to do so that you will get more benefit out of the medication?
- What percent, would you say, is the medicine doing its thing and what percent is of your doing?
- What do you need to do to increase the benefits of the medication?

Discussions initiated by these questions need to happen right from the beginning of treatment with medication and during each follow-up visit. The client should be repeatedly reminded that she needs to take an active role in getting herself to feel better.

CASE EXAMPLE: SOMETIMES THE CUSTOMER IS HIDDEN IN A DISABILITY CLAIM REQUEST

Unfortunately, the dually diagnosed individual commonly becomes dependent upon public assistance to make ends meet. When these individuals have drinking problems they must often attend treatment programs as a condition of continued disability payments. From a traditional treatment perspective, the clinician may be tempted to dismiss the client as unmotivated for real change and further the condition of continued disability payments upon strict adherence with program guidelines, such as abstinence. Though we do not disagree with abstinence as a reasonable goal, we do not believe coercion is an effective means to that end. Sometimes the clinician can "ignore" the problem altogether and focus on the client's picture of what his life is going to look like when the problems he has are gone. The following is an excerpt from a session Norm had with a man in his mid-thirties who came to therapy with two requests: "psychoactive" medication and a signature on his disability form.

The Miracle Question

NORM: Let me ask you a different question. Let's say tonight, in the middle of the night, a miracle occurred, and all the problems that have come with you today, they vanish, they are gone. But, because this miracle happens in the middle of the night, while you are sleeping, you can't know it has

---

Quick Tip:

Nurturing Change

When practiced consistently, small changes lead to big changes.

happened. What would you notice, first thing tomorrow, that would let you know this miracle had occurred?

BILL: I would be happy with myself, with the way conditions are and the way things are going.

NORM: Okay, and how would you tell you were happy?

BILL: I would be more responsible, more able to cope with situations. More happiness.

NORM: And when you noticed you were more responsive, more able to cope, what would you be doing?

Notice how quickly the client switches from the future tense of imagining what life without his problems would be like to realizing there are certain times now when he at least "acts" like he hasn't a problem in the world.

BILL: I will take care of the phone. I never thought about that before. I'll take care of the phone.

NORM: What else?

BILL: I can answer the phone or do other things like check the mail. I can do the chores around the house. Refinish a piece of furniture or rake the leaves.

NORM: Who else would notice you were living in this miracle day?

BILL: My wife, she'd know I'd be better off.

NORM: What would she notice that would tell her you were better off?

BILL: I would speak more directly to her.

By continuing in a positive and optimistic manner, this client was able to develop a detailed picture of what his life would look like the day after a miracle occurred. He was also able to point to several "exceptional" days when he was already living in a manner that indicated to him that he had not only made progress but also that more progress was possible.

CLIENTS WHO ARE HIV POSITIVE

Many times in our supervision of therapists working with clients who are HIV positive or who have AIDS, we have noticed a tendency on the part of the therapist to insist the client do her dying *by the book*. The traditional model of dying instructs the therapist to be on the lookout for the denial and bargaining stages of dying, to encourage the client's anger and depression through acting out and tears, while always aiming for the first signs of surrender and acceptance that are inevitably at the end of the grief.

We do not believe there is a right way to go about living with AIDS or dying from an opportunistic infection. We believe it is the therapist's job to be helpful to the client and therefore we continually ask, "How can I be helpful to you today?" To emphasize our position with the client we open most sessions as if they were the first session by asking, "What can we accomplish today that will let you know coming here to see me today is time well spent?" Phrasing our opening question in this manner is respectful of the client's limited amount of time and clearly communicates our willingness to help in whatever way we can.

Insoo met Liz, a remarkable young women who described her occupation as a "working girl" and had been suffering from AIDS for several years. Insoo spent a considerable amount of time finding out about this young woman's coping skills in her daily work with the johns. She listed in detail how she takes care of herself with the help of her one and only girlfriend. Where some might have advised her to give up such a hard life, Liz knew she must stay strong enough to work because it was her only source of income and independence. When Insoo asked the young woman about her miracle picture, she said that her miracle would be, "I will die well." Although shocked by this realistic answer, Insoo followed through by asking what she meant. After some thought, Liz finally formulated that it meant that her mother would finally find out that Liz turned out to be a "good person." She had not seen her mother in over 17 years; Liz left home as a teenage runaway after being told by nearly everyone she knew that she would never amount to anything because she was evil.

Insoo and Liz then discussed what it would take for her mother to find out that she turned out to be a "good person." The young women weighed several options, but finally decided to write her mother a letter explaining how she turned out to be a good person. As the session closed, the client thanked Insoo for not being like the other therapists she had seen who told her she would die in peace only if she returned to her hometown to confront her family, particularly her two brothers who had brutally sexually abused her. This client had the strength and good sense to know her own mind and refuse to follow the professionals' advice. We think it is respectful to allow a client to die in the manner she chooses, with dignity, self-respect, and in a way that fits her. We will always admire Liz for following her self-determined path.

Chapter 14
Women and Substance Use

The field of addiction treatment is becoming increasingly sensitive to women in recovery and their unique needs. Historically, the study and treatment of substance abuse, particularly alcohol, has been dominated by male professionals who studied primarily male abusive drinkers. The tendency of treatment has been skewed somewhat toward what makes sense in a male culture. For example, traditional treatment language, like *confrontation, hit hard on his denial*, and *tell him what reality is*, is consistent with the view that one must face the problem head on, by force if necessary, an approach that is clearly male-oriented. However, many clinical indicators show that women are not comfortable with the confrontational treatment approaches and prefer programs that appeal to women's approach to problem solving.

We are also learning that women's use and misuse of substances are very different than men's, as are their concerns and way of constructing solutions. In Japan, women drinkers are called "kitchen drinkers," which illustrates the degree and nature of this hidden problem as well as the shame that accompanies the secrecy. Unlike men, who can become violent or get into fights in a bar when drunk, women tend to hide their misuse and abuse, internalize their problems, and are devastated by the destruction of relationships and self-esteem. One women client we worked with described her evenings: "I was always alone. I'd get into bed with my bottle and a book. I would hide myself from everyone." As if this was not bad enough, when she finally entered treatment, she was made to wear a sign around her neck that said "bitchy" because she fought the treatment mandate that forbids clients from seeing their children.

We believe the treatment must be sensitive to the special needs of women. Women are more oriented toward relationship issues, caretaker roles, and responsibility for the childcare, and they have a stronger sense of the lack of control over their lives. They are also prone to blame themselves for their life circumstances and take responsibility for problems far beyond what is realistic and reasonable. When coupled with the marginal role most women play in financial and other decision-making issues, women feel more vulnerable and helpless. Therefore, treatment programs must address these issues with

The Issue of Shame

In recent years a great deal has been written about the issue of shame and how it is both a cause and result of problem drinking. Shame has been described as multigenerational (Bradshaw, 1988) and the cause of not only substance addictions but also the "behavioral addictions" as well. The usual remedy to this problem has been to get it out in the open and talk about it. It is our contention that this approach has its limitations. Sometimes talking on and on about shame has the effect of reinforcing the shame and making it worse. Because we are in the habit of listening to our clients and allowing them to teach us how to do therapy, we have learned a more creative way to help our clients deal with shame. This discovery happened when Insoo was working with a "closet drinker" who said she was very ashamed of her drinking. But her drinking was in the closet, no one knew about it—not family, not even her close friends. Insoo's client explained it was the shame at what she turned out to be that was the most painful for her. Insoo suddenly realized there was a big difference between the kind of person her client turned out to be and the kind of person she thought she was. Insoo explored this observation with her client and there was ready agreement. The discussion focused on how to bridge the gap, which of course included a sober life.

Shame can be looked at as a disconnection between the client's internal and external view of herself. This usually widens the distance between the client's internal and external view of himself. The therapeutic task then becomes how to connect these two different images.

This view of shame opens the door to questions about what the problem drinker thought of herself before the drinking became a problem (when then two views of herself were not so far apart) or to questions about how she can become more like the internal view of herself. Scaling questions can be helpful to determine where the client is today and what will be different when the next small step is taken. This is a much more optimistic and effective view of dealing with the issue of shame; it is easier to work with our clients to bridge the gap than to root the shame.

sensitivity. The best way to be sensitive is to *ask* women what they need to help their recovery along, then listen to them without preconceived ideas of what they need and without "reading between the lines" (de Shazer, 1995).

We have found that asking women about their relationships is very helpful. Women tend to be dependent on men and to feel more helpless about shaping their own lives than men do. By asking questions that focus on primary relationships, women begin to understand what their relationships are like and how they want them to change. Ask questions that point the client toward workable solutions and draw upon what she has already done to make her relationship healthier. Since relationships with their children are important to most mothers, we advocate that the children, even young children, play prominent roles in treatment. As we have mentioned all along, we do not think it is helpful to pathologize people or label them with negative roles. It is not helpful to round up all the children so that they can tell you how dysfunctional their mother has been. We think it is more helpful to find out from them what they have been doing to help their mother and to help them make the best of the situation. We support the idea that children are doing the best they can at all times and we want to find behaviors that they can keep doing.

Helplessness, a sense of a lack of control over her life, and decision making are also issues for women. We suggest that you raise these issues with questions, not by telling the client what to do. It is important to pay attention to how you phrase your questions. For example, listen to the following ways to ask about her sense of control. Since women are sensitive to relationship issues, it is productive to use many variations on the following questions.*

1. What kind of help would your husband say he needs from you so that he can become the kind of man you deserve to be married to?

2. What kind of help does your husband need from you so that he can communicate with you better?

3. What would he say he wants you to do so you are more helpful in his attempt to talk to you more?

4. What would your children say they would like you to keep doing that is helpful to them?

5. What kind of help do you need from your children, even a little?

6. What are the things you need to keep doing so that you can stay healthy?

7. What kind of help do you need from your husband?

8. What is the first small thing that he can do that is helpful to you?

---

*Our definition of a relationship includes both traditional and nontraditional relationships. Though we have used the traditional labels of husband and wife, we believe our questions are helpful for couples in nonmarital relationships as well as gay and lesbian relationships. We support these relationships and encourage you to to so also.

. . . .

Questions from the Field:

This is such simple stuff. How can it work with such a complex problem like substance abuse?"

Many people confuse our simple ideas with simple-mindedness. We have even heard the criticism that our ideas are so simple we must be in denial about substance abuse problems. We believe there is a great deal of complexity in simple ideas. Furthermore, it takes a great deal of discipline and clear-headedness to stay simple. Solution-focused therapy assumes that even a complicated problem begins to be resolved with a simple solution (one that is often overlooked by the client and by a therapist who is looking in the wrong direction).

9. What difference would it make to you when he actually does these things?

10. What is the best way you can allow your husband to be helpful to you?

Notice that these questions address the client's view of how others view her and how she can be helpful to those around her. To insist that the woman take care of herself would be such a foreign idea for her that it will diminish her strengths and reduce her to feeling like she is a failure in interpersonal aspects as well as in drinking. She views her life from a relationship orientation; it is her identity, and to strip it away at the beginning of treatment is a disservice. Instead, work with her strengths until she develops her own sense of who she is, what she wants to be, and then the tendency to "put others first" will be replaced with her ability to do nice things for herself.

CASE EXAMPLE: GRETA CAN STILL BE HELPFUL

Greta gave up her career when children were born 12 years ago, soon after marriage. She stayed home to raise her two boys. About eight years ago her husband started his own business and she helped with the bookkeeping. The business grew and required a more advanced and sophisticated level of business management, far superior to anything Greta could do. Not wanting to leave the children while she pursued more training, Greta gave up the job of helping her husband's business. As the business grew, her husband became more absorbed and consumed by the success of the business. Greta began to drink. Her drinking led to arguments and her husband would spend more and more time on the job instead of coming home to see his intoxicated wife. Her housekeeping and childcare standards slipped and she ended up in treatment when her husband threatened divorce. She told us later that she was in a fog most of the time and the best thing she did for herself was to agree to a detox program. While in detox she planned and outlined her first visit with the children, who were, she said, "everything to me." She decided to concentrate on spending time with the children, just enjoying them and having fun with them, and not be pressured about coming home soon.

When we asked the above questions of Greta, it was the first time anybody ever asked her how she can be *helpful* to her husband, a man who has always been so successful and competent during their entire marriage. Just by answering these questions Greta was able to see herself as being successful and competent in the marriage.

Unique approaches to problem solving for women include:
1. consensus-building approaches by eliciting everyone's opinion,
2. negotiation through give and take,
3. conciliatory approaches rather then confrontational approaches,
4. paying attention to personal issues and their personal meaning to women, and
5. use of tentative language and hedging in speech. Women use language that includes many words like *perhaps, could it be, I wonder.*

● ●

Tips from the field:

A Holistic Approach to Clients

There is more going on in the client's life than the substance abuse. Pay attention to what else she needs to pay attention to. This helps the client see that her life is more than substance abuse. When the therapist helps the client pay attention to the rest of her life, both strengths and weaknesses are discovered. The strengths can be used as additional solutions.

You will reach more women by using these relationship questions and tentative language in the beginning because they are consistent with a woman's way of thinking and speaking. Successful treatment is more likely if you view the issues from your client's perspective.

WHAT TO DO WHEN NOTHING SEEMS TO WORK

We all encounter cases that test our stamina, challenge our skills, and make us wonder why we became therapists in the first place. Clients who seem determined to destroy themselves, who can't seem to get their life together, however hard those around them try—including us—can make us feel like throwing the book at them and screaming, "How dare you throw away your talent, personality, intellect, and future!" Before you do what we only think about doing, or worse, simply give up on the "hopeless cases," there is one more thought we would like to offer.

Whenever we are faced with such a case, we must remind ourselves that perhaps, however destructive it is for her right now, this may be the perfect spot for her at this point in her life. Maybe she is not ready for our positive and optimistic view of the future. Perhaps she will be ready tomorrow. We never know. To go one step further, it seems important to remind ourselves that she has to be at this place right now before she can move on to the next place. She has to go through what she is going through, right now, in order to get to her next place. When looked at this way, it becomes clear that however destructive it is now, she needs to be here.

With this perspective, we are able to respect her need to take her time and do what she needs to do for now. This is called acceptance and it is the essence of the "serenity prayer."

• • • • • • • • • • • • • • • • • • •

Tips from the Field:

Childcare and Transportation

For the majority of poor women, childcare and transportation remain the biggest obstacle to gaining success in treatment. Programs must recognize that women need childcare in order to come to the treatment and either provide childcare or help her create a concrete and feasible plan that provides care for her children.

Afterword: Confusion Is Our Best Product

We hear some amazing stories from our clients. Some stories are incredibly tragic and move us to tears. Some are so comical we are tempted to laugh out loud, but don't.

While incarcerated, one of Norm's clients attended an educational program on dysfunctional families that included descriptions of the family addict, enabler, hero, scapegoat, lost child, and mascot. Upon his release he shared his dissatisfaction with being his family's "escaping goat" and concluded it was time for him to escape his crime-infested neighborhood. His successful plan included moving from the north to south end of town, attending trade school, and marrying to his long-time girlfriend (who had stood by him because she saw his potential to "escape" his negative family influence).

Our final story comes from Insoo. She was seeing a man who had failed to keep his appointment eleven times. This made sense in light of his probation officer's demand that he show up for treatment of cocaine abuse even while the man insisted he was innocent. When the client showed positive results on a test for cocaine, Insoo calmly asked him how he explained his positive test while he swore he was clean. The man was silent for a long time, then finally reached down into his creative side and came up with an answer. He said he had this bunch of guys who came over and insisted on using his house to do drugs. Of course they used his glasses to drink water, beer, or whatever. The only way he could explain his positive test was that he must have used the same glasses that his cocaine buddies drank out of. Insoo, with a confused look, asked the man, "Wow, you never know these days what can happen. How do you suppose that happened?" The client was at a loss for words and then he started to confess that, well, maybe he used just a little bit of cocaine.

References

Children's Protective Services. (1996). *A strategy for change.* Lansing, MI: Family Independence Agency.

American Society of Addiction Medicine, Inc. (1996). *Patient placement criteria for the treatment of substance-related disorders* (2nd ed.). Chevy Chase, MD: Author.

Anderson, H., & Goolishan, H. (1992). The client is the expert: A non-knowing approach to therapy. In S. McNamee & K. J. Gregen (Eds.), *Therapy as social construction* (pp. 25–39). London: Sage.

Berg, I. K. (1994). *Family based services.* New York: Norton.

Berg, I. K., & Miller, S. D. (1992). *Working with problem drinkers: A solution-focused approach.* New York: Norton.

Blackborn, C. (1995, November/December). Relapse and the family. *The counselor,* 11–20.

Bradshaw, J. (1998). *Bradshaw on the family: A revolutionary way of self-discovery.* Pompano Beach, FL: Pompano Beach Health Communications.

Bruner, C. (1995). *Child abuse and child protection.* Des Moines, IA: Child and Family Policy Center.

Cabié, M.-C., (1995). Psychiatrie adulte san lits [Adult outpatient psychiatry]. *Therapie Familiale, 16*(1), 39–47.

Cantwell, P., & Holmes, S. (1994). Social construction: A paradigm shift for systemic therapy and training. *Australian & New Zealand Journal of Family Therapy, 15*(1), 17–26.

DeJong, P., & Berg, I. K. (1997). *Interviewing for solutions.* Pacific Grove: Brooks/Cole.

de Shazer, S. (1985). *Keys to solutions in brief therapy.* New York: Norton.

de Shazer, S. (1988). *Clues: Investigating solutions in brief therapy.* New York: Norton.

de Shazer, S. (1991). *Putting difference to work.* New York: Norton.

de Shazer, S., & Berg, I. K. (1992). Doing therapy: A post-structural re-vision. *Journal of Marital and Family Therapy, 18*(1), 71–81.

de Shazer, S. (1995). *Words were originally magic.* New York: Norton.

Foy, D. W., Nunn, L. B., & Rychtarik, R. G. (1984). Broad-spectrum behavioral treatment for chronic alcoholics: Effects of training controlled drinking skills. *Journal of Consulting and Clinical Psychology, 52,* 218–230.

Furman, B., & Ahola, T. (1992). *Solution talk: Hosting therapeutic conversations.* New York: Norton.

Haley, J., (1993). *On Milton Erickson.* New York: Brunner/Mazel.

Hester, R., & Miller, W. (1989). *Handbook of alcoholism treatment approaches: Effective alternatives.* New York: Pergamon.

Howard, K. I., Kopta, S. M., Krause, M. J., & Orlinsky, D. E. (1986). The dose effect relationship in psychotherapy. *American psychologist, 41,* 159–164.

Isebaert, L., & Cabié, M.-C. (1997). *Le croix comme ethique precis pratique de therapie dite "breve"* (Ethical choices in brief therapy). Paris: Toulous Eres.

Johnson, V. E. (1973). *I'll quit tomorrow.* New York: Harper & Row.

Martin, J. (1992). *Chalk talk on alcoholism* [Film]. Center City, MN: Hazelton.

Orford, J., & Edwards, G. (1977). *Alcoholism: A comparison of treatment and advice with a study of the influence of marriage.* Oxford: Oxford University.

Orford, J. (1985). *Excessive appetites: A psychological view of addictions.* New York: Wiley.

Sanchez-Craig, M. (1993). *Saying when: How to quit drinking or cut down.* Toronto: Addiction Resource Foundation.

Sobell, L. C., Sobell, M. B., Toneatto, T., & Leo, G. (1993). What triggers the resolution of alcohol problems without treatment? *Alcoholism: Clinical and Experimental Research 17*(2).

Sobell, M. B., & Sobell, L. C. (1978). *Behavioral treatment of alcohol problems: Individualized therapy and controlled drinking.* New York: Plenum.

Talmon, M. (1990). *Single-session therapy: Maximizing the effect of the first (and often only) therapeutic encounter.* San Francisco: Jossey-Bass.

Taube, C. A., Burns, B. J., & Kessler, L. (1984). Patients of psychiatrists and psychologists in office-based practice: 1980. *American Psychologist, 39,* 1435–1447.

White, M., & Epston, D. (1990). *Narrative means to therapeutic ends.* New York: Norton.

Appendix

SUBSTANCE USER'S COMPETENCY WORKSHEET

Name _____ Date _____

START HERE if you continue to use substances (alcohol and/or drugs), then skip to question 5

1. When are you now able to manage your use of substances even though it would be easy to overuse or abuse them?

2. How did you accomplish that? (List three things you did to get started.)

START HERE if you have decided to stop using substances, then proceed to question 5

3. When are you now able to refuse the use of substances even though they are available (without much effort) for you to use?

4. How do you accomplish this? (List three things you did to get started.)

5. How do these activities help you not drink or cut down on your use?

6. Who else notices that you are trying to make progress?

7. What would they say you have done that explains this progress you have made?

8. Suppose you decide to do even more of what is already working; in three months what will you be doing that you are not doing now?

9. What will other people notice that will explain this continued progress?

10. What will you do today to keep this progress going?

SUBSTANCE USER'S RECOVERY CHECKLIST AND WORKSHEET

NAME: _____ DOB: _____

Please answer each question with an "X" in the column to the right that best fits.
If a question does not pertain to you, place "N/A" in the column headed "NEVER."

I. MANAGE/ELIMINATE SUBSTANCE USE *(If you continue to use substances [drugs/alcohol], start here.)*	NEVER	1	2	3	4	5	ALWAYS
1. Able to place a limit on my use and not exceed that limit							
2. Able to consistently reduce my use of substances							
3. Able to eliminate my use for specific time periods							
4. Able to avoid situations where I might abuse substances							
(If you have decided to stop, start here.)							
5. Able to avoid situations where I might be tempted to use substances again							
6. Accepted my substance-free lifestyle							
7. Able to enjoy life without substances							
8. Able to recognize my substance-related lifestyle							
9. Comfortable socializing where substances are available without using and/or							
10. Able to leave situations (to protect my recovery) where substances are being used.							
II. EMOTIONAL, PSYCHOLOGICAL, & PHYSICAL WELL-BEING	NEVER	1	2	3	4	5	ALWAYS
1. Able to practice personal hygiene skills							
2. Able to relax without using substances							
3. Able to attend to physical health problems							
4. Able to put past problems in a positive perspective							
5. Able to express my feelings appropriately							
6. Able to admit mistakes to myself and others							
7. Participate in regular exercise							
8. Able to cope with stress (without substance use)							
9. Able to experience a positive self-image							
III. SOCIAL & FAMILY WELL-BEING	NEVER	1	2	3	4	5	ALWAYS
1. Able to maintain interest in welfare of others							
2. Able to maintain interest in family mambers							
3. Able to engage in social/family activities without substances							
4. Able to help with household chores							
5. Able to participate in child-rearing chores							
6. Able to communicate with significant other							
7. Able to solve problems with people							
8. Able to seek the support of family/friends							

continued

IV. JOB AND FINANCIAL WELL-BEING	NEVER	1	2	3	4	5	ALWAYS
1. Able to go to work							
2. Able to improve job performance							
3. Able to maintain a balanced household budget							
4. Able to budget time to accomplish tasks							
5. Able to use talents and abilities to better myself							

V. SPIRITUAL WELL-BEING	NEVER	1	2	3	4	5	ALWAYS
1. Able to have an interest in my own future							
2. Able to experience a sense of peacefulness							
3. Able to maintain a positive outlook on life							
4. Able to experience and express gratitude							

GOAL WORKSHEET

Four or fewer areas (from the above left) where a little improvement will make a big difference.

1. _____

2. _____

3. _____

4. _____

How will improvement in these areas make a difference in your use of substancees (drugs and alcohol)?

_____

_____

_____

_____

_____

_____

_____

_____

_____

_____

SUCCESS PREDICTION SCALE

Directions: Please indicate your clinical impression in each of the following eight domains.

1. What does your client want to accomplish in therapy?

3 stop drinking/drugging
2 cut down on drinking/drugging
1 reduce the harm of current use of drugs/alcohol
1 other

2. Is your client's goal a workable goal for therapy?

3 yes
2 yes, with modifications
1 no

3. What is the client-therapist relationship?

3 customer type
2 complainer type
1 visitor type

4. Does the client have resources that can be used to meet the goal of treatment?

(consider time, energy, money, motivation, people, skills)

4 many
3 some
2 few
1 none

5. Is the client willing to make the changes necessary to meet the goal of therapy?

4 ready now
3 somewhat ready
2 will be ready soon
1 not ready now
0 will never be ready

6. Are there previous attempted solutions (including previous treatment) that your client thinks are applicable to the current goal of therapy?

3 applicable
2 somewhat applicable
0 not applicable

7. Did your client experience success as a result of these previous attempts at a solution?

3 successful
2 somewhat successful
1 not successful

8. Are comorbid difficulties present?

4 none
3 mild
2 moderate
1 severe

_____Total Rating

SOLUTION-FOCUSED SESSION NOTE

Client's Name _____

DOB _____ Clinic ID # _____

PROBLEM (*problem statement in the client's own words*)

For a first-session note, describe the problem that brings the client into therapy in the client's own words. Also include the client's self-assessment of the severity of the problem upon entering therapy with a problem scale. In second and later sessions, simply indicate "same" when working on the same problem; if the client decides to work on an additional problem, describe that problem in the client's own words.

EXCEPTIONS/PROGRESS (*presession change, exceptions, miracle day behaviors, solutions, indications that it's better*)

Record a detailed description of exceptions and indicate progress by noting the client's self-assessment on progress scales.

MESSAGE (*compliments and thoughts on solutions*)

Record compliments, educational information you may have provided, and solutions that either the client has developed or you have suggested.

HOMEWORK (*tasks that are either original to the client or that involve doing more of what is already working*)

In a first-session note, describe the homework assignment. In second and later sessions, use this section to indicate either a continuation of the previous session's homework or a new homework assignment.

Date _____ Diagnosis _____ Clinician_____

WEEKLY WORKSHEET

NAME: _____

What will be different about you when you finish this course and are no longer a drinking driver?

WEEKLY WORKSHEET

NAME: _____

When did you drink and not drive?

How did you do that?

How will you know you can do that every time you drink?

WEEKLY WORKSHEET

NAME: _____

Please consider this situation. A fellow goes into a bar after work and orders a beer. He slowly drinks the beer and as he approaches the bottom of the glass the bartender notices and asks, "Do you want a refill?" The fellow looks up and says, "No thanks, I'm driving." Your question for this week is: HOW DOES HE DO THIS?

WEEKLY WORKSHEET

NAME: _____

What have you done this week to lower your risks for future DWI arrests?

WEEKLY WORKSHEET

NAME: _____

What will your (spouse, parent, child, friend, life partner) be doing differently when he or she gets the idea that he or she no longer needs to worry about your getting into trouble?

1.

2.

3

4.

5.

WEEKLY WORKSHEET

NAME: _____

How do you know your drinking is moderate when you are a moderate drinker?

OR

Eight rules you would suggest people follow to be moderate drinkers:

1.

2.

3.

4.

5.

6.

7.

8.

WEEKLY WORKSHEET

NAME: _____

Imagine it is one year from today. You have become a nondrinking driver. What have you done to prevent a backslide?

WEEKLY WORKSHEET

NAME: _____

For this experience (arrest, court appearance, alcohol use evaluation, counseling, fines, license reinstatement fees, legal fees) to make a difference in your life, something must be different, or this experience is just another damned thing. What is that something that is different AND how do you know it's different?

WEEKLY WORKSHEET

NAME: _____

How are you different when you switch off the desire to drink alcohol and do something else?

WEEKLY WORKSHEET

NAME: _____

Before your driver's license can be returned you must sign the following statement.

"I believe that I have attained sufficient progress in treatment so that I can and will avoid future drinking-driving offenses."

In what specific wats have you made changes that you can now consider yourself a nondrinking driver?

1.

2.

3.

4.

5.

6.

7.

8.

9.

10.

ALTERNATE
WEEKLY WORKSHEET

1. What have you done since your arrest/conviction to lower your risk for a future DWI arrest?

2. How did you do these things?

3. How did doing these things help you?

4. Who else has noticed you are trying to make progress?

5. What would they say you have done that explains this progress you have made?

6. Suppose you decided to do even more of what you have already begun; in three months, what will you be doing that you are not doing now?

7. What will other people notice that will explain this continued progress?

COUPLES IN RECOVERY CHECKLIST

NAME:_____ DOB:_____

Please answer each question with an "X" in the column to the right that best fits.
If a question does not pertain to you, place "N/A" in the column headed "JUST A LITTLE."

	JUST A LITTLE	MORE THAN ½	VERY MUCH
1. HOUSEHOLD MANAGEMENT			
• SHARE HOUSEHOLD CHORES/YARD CLEANING			
• SHOW SPIRIT OF COOPERATION			
• SOLVE PROBLEMS WITHOUT BLAMING			
2. FINANCIAL MANAGEMENT			
• AGREE ON HOW TO SPEND MONEY			
• HAVE A SYSTEM OF MAKING DECISIONS ON MONEY			
• AGREE ON WHAT IS IMPORTANT TO US FINANCIALLY			
3. CHILDREN / RELATIVE ISSUES			
• AGREE ON VALUES TO TEACH OUR CHILD(REN)			
• SHARE CHILDCARE RESPONSIBILITIES			
• ATTEND ACTIVITIES OF CHILDREN (SCHOOL, SPORTS, ETC.)			
• IN-LAWS BELIEVE I AM A GOOD PARTNER			
4. EMOTIONAL / RELATIONSHIPS			
• ARE COOPERATIVE SEXUAL PARTNERS			
• SHARE/EXPRESS "WE ARE IN THIS FOR THE LONG HAUL"			
• LEAVE THE PAST IN THE PAST			
• ARE MORE THAN PARTNERS; WE ARE FRIENDS			
• DISAGREE RESPECTFULLY			
5. RECREATION / FUN			
• PLAN VACATIONS, OUTINGS, FUN TOGETHER			
• TAKE TIME FOR JOINT ACTIVITIES (WALKS, MOVIES, DINNER, ETC.)			
• PRACTICE RITUALS AND TRADITION			
• ABLE TO LAUGH (AT ME AND WITH EACH OTHER)			
6. SPIRITUAL			
• BELIEVE IN EACH OTHER'S GOODNESS AND GOODWILL			
• WANT TO LEAVE THIS WORLD A BETTER PLACE			
• SHARE A POSITIVE, CONFIDENT OUTLOOK FOR THE FUTURE			
• BELIEVE WE ARE BETTER WITH EACH OTHER THAN ALONE			

From the above list, indicate three areas where a little improvement would make a difference:

1. _____ _____

2. _____

3. _____

Based upon the work of Steve de Shazer, Insoo Kim Berg, and the Brief Therapy Center, Milwaukee, Wisconsin.

Index

•••

Two books by Insoo Kim Berg and Scott D. Miller devoted
specifically to helping the problem drinker

THE MIRACLE METHOD: A RADICALLY NEW APPROACH TO PROBLEM DRINKING

by Scott D. Miller and Insoo Kim Berg
(0-393-31533-9, 192 pages, paper)

This book is written for your clients and for those who know they have a drinking problem and are ready to do something about it. In a practical and conversational style, the authors explain their radically new and effective approach to problem drinking. They invite the reader to "discover the resources and strengths that you possess right now that can be used to bring about the changes you desire. That is what the miracle method is all about: rallying your own strengths and resources in order to solve your problems with alcohol" (from chapter 1).

> "At last! A how-to book that describes a tailor-made approach to each individual rather than a 'one size fits all' recovery formula. *The Miracle Method* provides a way for each person to create his own vision of success and the path he needs to follow to get there.
>
> "As a clinician who has worked with substance abusers for twenty years, I feel this book provides a dramatically useful alternative to the disease model of addiction. Some of my clients and I are using the method already with startlingly positive results. I only wish that I had this powerful treatment tool years ago.
>
> "Expect miracles!"
>
> —David Treadway, Ph.D.
> Author, *Before It's Too Late: Working with Substance Abuse in the Family*

WORKING WITH THE PROBLEM DRINKER: A SOLUTION-FOCUSED APPROACH

by Insoo Kim Berg and Scott D. Miller
(0-393-70134-4, 224 pages, cloth)

"It's a miracle! Finally, a wellness-oriented book about alcohol abuse treatment that capitalizes on client strengths and resources and invites the client to identify the goals for treatment. . . . this is an excellent practice-oriented book."
> —*Journal of Family Psychotherapy*

Published by W. W. Norton & Company, Inc.

To order, call 1-800-233-4830

•••

Notes

Notes

Notes

Notes

Notes

Notes